MW01591296

THE OPENING WAY

Kurozumi Munetada,
Founder of Kurozumikyō

Kurozumi Tadaaki

Translated by Julie Iezzi
and Harold Wright
with assistance from Kamiya Sumio

Edited by Willis Stoesz
Wright State University

UNIVERSITY
PRESS OF
AMERICA

Lanham • New York • London

Copyright © 1994 by
University Press of America®, Inc.
4720 Boston Way
Lanham, Maryland 20706

3 Henrietta Street
London WC2E 8LU England

Library of Congress Cataloging-in-Publication Data

Kurozumi, Tadaaki.
[Kyōsoden. English]
The opening way : Kurozumi Munetada, founder of Kurozumikyō /
by Kurozumi Tadaaki ; translated by Julie Iezzi and Harold Wright
with assistance from Kamiya Sumio ; edited by Willis Stoesz.
p.   cm.
1. Kurozumi, Munetada, 1780–1850.   2. Kurozumikyō (Religious
organization)—Biography.   I. Stoesz, Willis.
BL2222.K8892K88613   1994
299'.5619—dc20   94–16763 CIP
[B]

ISBN 0–8191–9574–X (cloth : alk. paper)
ISBN 0–8191–9575–8 (pbk. : alk. paper)

 The paper used in this publication meets the minimum requirements of
American National Standard for Information Sciences—Permanence
of Paper for Printed Library Materials, ANSI Z39.48–1984.

Portrait of the Founder by Takeda Gohou

Contents

Figures

Editor's Preface

My first contact with the subject of this book came early one midwinter morning in Okayama, Japan. I was serving as an exchange professor, and a colleague had asked if I would like to observe an interesting Shinto ritual. Immediately I agreed. I spoke very little Japanese, but I was eager to learn and ready for the unexpected.

A few days later a young man appeared at my door in the predawn hours, and together we drove out of the city to a nearby hill. Curving roads on a hillside led to a graceful set of buildings. All was new and smelled of cedar. Soon we went out, up a short path to where a large wooden platform was set at the very top of the hill. A few tall pine trees stood about in the gathering light. A number of people assembled, sitting Japanese-style on cushions in rows, facing the east.

Soon a dignified, vigorous-looking man appeared and seated himself at the front of the platform, facing directly the point on the horizon where the sun would soon rise. He began a chant which continued to the moment the sun's disk appeared. Then all present made sounds of taking in air through their mouths, and there was silence. A lovely, lilting tune was sung, evidently a chant of praise to the rising sun. The mood of the group was reverent, but I sensed the brief ceremony was deeply familiar to them all, part of a settled pattern.

I had taken part in *Nippai,* a service of worship before the rising sun. It is a ritual based directly on the life and thought of the group's founder. His name was Kurozumi Munetada (1780-1850), and I was a guest of the Shinto denomination Kurozumikyō. Presiding at *Nippai* was The Reverend Kurozumi Muneharu, the Sixth Patriarch *(Kyōshu)* of the group and a direct descendant of the founder.

During my stay in Okayama I returned a number of times to Shintozan

("Shinto Mountain"), as the headquarters on the hilltop is called. I found that the good-smelling wood used for the buildings was *hinoki,* tradition-ally used for Shinto shrines including the important Ise Shrine. Their graceful style is a modern statement of traditional Japanese architecture. Students from our own university were entertained at Shintozan as part of a summer exchange program with a local university, and our friendship continued to ripen. The early morning winter visit was the beginning of a series of events that has led to this biography of Kurozumi Munetada appearing in English.

In that time I have seen that The Reverend Kurozumi has an abiding interest in making Shinto better understood. When I left Okayama a representative of the *Kyōshu* saw me off at the station, bearing a "travel safely" gift and hinting that perhaps we might meet again in my own country. I took the hint seriously, and after many negotiations a party of three leaders of Kurozumikyō took part with a number of American experts in Japanese religion in a "Conference on Kurozumi Shinto" in Dayton, Ohio. By then it was April, 1985.

Professors Helen Hardacre and H. Byron Earhart gave major presenta-tions in addition to several by the Reverend Kurozumi himself. The concluding session featured Shinto and Christian prayers and presenta-tions on the topic of world peace from the two perspectives. Joining the Reverend Kurozumi was Father Bertrand Buby, at that time Provincial of the Cincinnati Province of the Society of Mary.

These efforts to open Shinto viewpoint to broader understanding still continue. The Reverend Kurozumi's conference presentations, plus two other articles of his, were published in 1989 along with poetry of the founder and articles by several specialists in Japanese religion who had attended.[1] A year later, Kurozumikyō sponsored a conference at Shintozan for an executive committee of the Global Forum. A group of religious and parliamentary leaders from around the world were introduced to Japanese religion in Shinto perspective. Now, this biography of the founder becoming available is the most recent step.

There is about Shinto a direct and sincere confidence in the goodness of the human spirit. The austerity and dignity of its ritual and its architecture cannot but elevate the spirit of anyone whose eyes and ears are open. The inner springs of health and of healthy interaction with others are plumbed by its teaching. Its purity of spirit encourages those who seek inner simplicity; those who would be knowers of such purity can be glad to be found in such company.

However, *The Opening Way* gives us no plaster saint. The founder was a man who struggled with the imperfections he saw in himself. Though he dedicated himself at an early age to excellence in spiritual life, that excellence did not come easily. A crisis at the time of the death of his parents undermined the faith of his early manhood; and even after his profound conversion and the beginnings of his success in helping others, he found he needed to reach deeper within. His eyes were always on Amaterasu the great Kami of the Sun, whose presence within himself drew him on.

What is Shinto?

There are many for whom the very term "Shinto" communicates little. Images of a war fought a half-century ago linger in our minds, often mingling with impressions of Japan's more recent economic success, disconcerting to some Americans and causing speculation about what enabled such a "postwar miracle." Most of these leftover images stem from a version of Shinto that was a passing phase ending in 1945, known as State Shinto. What we see in *The Opening Way* has little to do with that, and much more with a way of life with roots in history and in community. We see, in fact, a man of peace and of personal culture with a strong concern for others. He was a man from times when modern strains had not yet torn society in many directions, a man of faith whose life still offers lessons for us today.

Broadly, "Shinto" refers to the historic belief of Japanese people in countless spiritual presences, known as kami, dwelling in mountains and rivers and in the land, expressing the beauty of the landscape and enlivening the crops, and to their interaction with these kami.[2] Other kami are ancestors of clans or heroes of the past, and still others are known through the ancient mythology of the Japanese people. They are worshiped in shrines scattered throughout the landscape and in the cities. Some of these shrines have regional and even national significance and are staffed by priestly families whose origins are in the distant past, but many are minded by local volunteers who treasure for their neighborhoods this access to mystery, good fortune, and personal renewal.

A few of the kami began as individuals who were masterful healers and teachers, people who turned their insight into human ill and good into ways of living for others. The most outstanding of these became founders of movements whose followers formed organizations ("sects" or "denominations") that have stood the test of time.

There are thus a number of sorts of Shinto, ranging from local folk beliefs to official expressions of national identity. Its origins lie in prehistoric times. Through the centuries Buddhist and Confucian beliefs have mingled with it, enriching Japanese culture with important resources of ethical beliefs, poetry, and ritual. While much of this was stimulated by periodic influxes from China, much flowered in Japan through the life of its own people and from its own distinctive insight.

During the late Tokugawa period (1600-1867), as the social fabric was strained by changing times and sensitive spirits felt uneasy, there were movements for renewal, for finding fresh forms of spiritual strength. Founders of these movements formulated ways of practice and belief that promised hope for people who felt need. One of these, among the earliest of them, was the man whose biography we have before us, Kurozumi Munetada.

There are books about Japan that tell this story in general perspective,[3] but this biography lets us know what that renewal meant to the people themselves. More than this, Kurozumikyō carries forward his vision of things today, in the life of the members of its local churches and in the contacts its leaders are making in recent years.

As the Meiji period (1867-1912) began, the leadership of Japan was taken over by a new generation which was intent on making of Japan a modern nation, able to hold its own with other nations. What we call "State Shinto" was an ingenious policy by which Japan's nineteenth-century government sought to marshal a vibrant, closely-knit people into a global power.[4]

Kurozumi Munetada was a man of a generation before that, of times before a corps of administrators narrowed Shinto down into an educational program that would serve the purposes of national development. From the life of Kurozumi Munetada we gain a rather different appreciation of Shinto than could ever come from knowing only the martial strictures of wartime State Shinto, or the ethos of a postwar success-oriented cohort of economic leaders. Shinto, better understood, draws on a broad range of values and rituals from across Japanese cultural history that are rooted closely in the life of ordinary people.

A Man with a Mission

Kurozumi Munetada was a man with a mission, and that mission moved toward a universal horizon. "Mission" is a concept we ordinarily associate with western religion and western society. We think of missionaries committed to spreading the Christian gospel, or of military or marketing organizations with specific tasks to accomplish. It is a concept with deep roots in western thinking, drawing on beliefs in an original creation of the world and a last judgement of the world toward which God, the Lord of history, directs human events. What "mission" might mean in Japanese culture, formed by rather different assumptions, might be a bit of a mystery.

But it becomes much less a mystery when we have seen the close attention Munetada gave to his own inner spiritual condition, and the care he gave to his healing activity and to the spiritual guidance of those who came to him for help. The concepts we see him using allow us to understand some distinctively Japanese patterns of urgency and commitment. His vow to become a "living kami" devoted to the health of others, and the mandate he received from Amaterasu in his own climactic experience of being healed, are basic to our understanding.

At age 20 he made a vow to become a "living kami" *(ikigami)*. Adopting such a goal was by no means common. Ordinarily a Japanese person would expect to become a kami only after death, and that through the rituals of remembrance his surviving family would devote to the purification of his spirit.[5] Munetada's approach brought heaven down to earth; he sought full purity of inner spirit in the here and now. His initial means to this goal was constant self-examination by five criteria he set for himself, and his purpose was to bring honor to his parents (Chapter 2).

However, twelve years later his parents died in quick succession. With his life-purpose shattered, his health deteriorated to such a degree that he was expected not to live. At this point he shifted the scope of his commitment, projecting it beyond his expected death and vowing that even after death he would be a kami bestowing healing on all who would need it. Then, unexpectedly, his health began to return when it dawned on him that at the deepest level his life derived not from his parents who had begotten him, but from Amaterasu the Kami of the Sun. He should experience his life as a gift from Amaterasu, making gratitude to her and not ethical striving the mainspring of his life's purpose (Chapter 3).[6]

The character of his vow thus underwent a 180-degree shift, from an action intensely his own initiative to one that was receptive in fundamental mood. Any perfection he might have thought he could achieve, he now saw had already been achieved in the infinite goodness of Amaterasu. He saw with increasing clarity that he should honor the presence of the Kami within himself by bringing every moment of his life into harmony with it, both his actions in relation to others and his every thought in his inner heart *(kokoro)*.[7] The moment of union left him with a mandate, a mission that became increasingly clear to him as he attended to the needs of others (Chapter 4). It was a mandate that directed his attention both inward to his own self-understanding, leading to renewed efforts to become more selfless in daily actions (Chapter 5), and outward in compassion to the tension and pain others around him were feeling. He understood this impulsion within himself through the Confucian concept of the "Mandate of Heaven" *(tenmei jikiju)*. His transformative experience is referred to as "The Direct Bestowal of Divine Mission."

"Mission" implies no political goal. Its special character is made clear by the renewed efforts he put forth to become more selfless within, at a time when the response from others to his teaching began to flag (Chapter 5). The rituals he employed as spiritual exercises *(shugyō)* were drawn from contemporary devotional practice, but his use of them was designed to render himself more selfless and more attentive to others' innermost needs.

His experience of divine mandate was for him the highest source of value in life, so that all other values became subject to it. Amaterasu was for him an inwardly perceived reality, transcendent to all else that could be known by which one might be otherwise tempted to live.[8] She was for him the Cosmic Spirit *(honshin)*, and within his own heart *(kokoro)* was a "divided portion" *(bunshin)* of that Spirit.

Bringing every moment of his life into unity with that inner presence, and therefore with the Cosmic Spirit animating the universe as a whole, was the agenda to which he set himself as a life-long task. At the same time, he threw his energies into preaching and healing, and his followers continued to spread his teachings after his death. There was no limit to those who would benefit from Amaterasu's enlivening presence. Kurozumi spirituality is both urgent and universal in its fundamental intention.

In the time of its first success, during the closing decades of the nineteenth century, Kurozumikyō was very close to the cultural currents drawn on by the Meiji period builders of modern Japan in uniting its people. Its focus on Amaterasu, who is also the patron deity of the Imperial family, had that effect. Today, after the vicissitudes of the twentieth century, Kurozumikyō has recovered its universal spiritual heritage. Its leaders seek to engage western readers in a sense of global partnership.

The Founder's Understanding of Health

There is a further point we should not overlook. Munetada's life and thought contribute to our western discussion of what a more "natural" approach to health and healing might require. How, after all, might one put together a "wholistic" way of living? What structure should it have, what kind of personal discipline is needed, what should be its sources in ultimate reality and its relation to ethical concerns?

His view is that wholeness must be based in a spiritual encounter with the one source of all of life, Amaterasu the Kami of the Sun. His lifelong practice of inner unity with Amaterasu the Creator of all⁰ was the source of his rich practical insight into other people's inner pain and confusion, and of his ability to heal their spirits and therefore their bodies. Bodily health must be an expression of spiritual health.

Equally important, individuals' health should be part of a larger pattern, potentially a worldwide circle of interaction, based in the order Amaterasu gives to the daily circle of life, and finally to all that lives. The Way of Amaterasu, central to his teaching, puts health in perspective both of the inner life and of the environment in its near-range social world and in its broadest horizons.

For these reasons, and for other reasons readers will discover for themselves, the biography of Kurozumi Munetada rewards our attention. He was an educator of the Japanese spirit into an affirmative and universal way of thinking.

Where Does All This Leave Us?

Some suggestions about where this book leaves us may be helpful. How may we "place" the founder in terms of other knowledge? A few "outsider" kinds of suggestions can be given, relating the Kurozumi circle of faith to its historical setting; these need to be balanced from an "insider" viewpoint.[10]

Historically and socially, the founder of Kurozumikyō was a man of the late Tokugawa (Edo) period (1600-1867). His life was lived in Okayama in western Japan, halfway between Osaka and Hiroshima. Politically, Okayama was part of the Bizen domain, ruled firmly and judiciously by the Ikeda clan committed to Confucian virtues. He was a man of culture of samurai background, educated locally and in conversation with local intelligentsia.[11]

It was a time when many people still observed social class conventions and knew what place they were supposed to have in society. However, it is important to note the turbulence of the period. Recent research has been showing that social conflict was much more common in Japan than many scholars, emphasizing its homogeneity and harmony, have led us to realize. The Japan-wide growth of the pilgrimage to Ise, historic seat of the worship of Amaterasu, was a major expression of this conflict.[12]

Social currents of the day suggested changes in the offing, though most could not see the direction those changes would take. Rural unrest, growing economic pressure on the traditionally dominant samurai class, and the emergence of a relatively well-off urban population while the numbers of the poor and the needy increased, led many sensitive observers to say that a new age needed to dawn. Many were convinced that the Tokugawa government had been discredited, but no alternative to its governing power had as yet emerged.

Munetada was himself an active proponent of the Ise pilgrimage. However, his role was rather different from most of those involved in this complex phenomenon. Our biography emphasizes his empathy for the poor and needy people that he knew. The strong spiritual commitment people saw in him made him an important source of stability for many. Kurozumi faith grew as much from the ethos of such a time of uncertainty as it did from his inner experience; he was recognized as a founder of a marvelous source of renewal in discouraging and difficult times. Our text shows us the character of the founder's experience and takes us to the early stages of the formation of Kurozumikyō tradition in the early Meiji period.

We may also see Kurozumi Munetada in context of religious history. He was a founder in the full sense, though with Japanese qualifications of that helpful interpretive concept. He was a teacher, able to engender in others the same experience by which he himself had benefitted.

His zeal to perfection in a Confucian ethical sense was tempered by his awareness of the transcendent presence of the Sun Kami; his utter confidence in the Sun Kami emerged as humility and spontaneity; his experience of being healed of mortal illness gave him insight into others' illnesses of spirit. He was well practiced in various religious disciplines and devotions, most of which were familiar in traditional Shinto usage, but he based his use of them in his own strong experience of non-dualism. The keen edge he applied to his developing inner spirit was the thought of non-self *(mushin)*. His grace and buoyancy provide a new appreciation of the effects of these insights so basic to Asian cultures.

However, for those inside the Kurozumi circle of faith, such general considerations may be interesting but hardly the main point. For them, he is absolutely singular and different from other human beings. He attained complete unity with Amaterasu, and thus, above all others, he shows what being a human is all about. He has in fact become Munetada Kami, the one who fulfilled his vow of becoming able to heal anyone who would turn to him. He is the completely reliable guide to finding that ultimate happiness which everyone seeks. His help may be sought and received in prayer; stories about him can illuminate others' search for self-understanding.

Those whose lives have been shaped by following his Way reverence him as their best possible teacher, the one who has shown them the way to cross over all difficulties that may arise in their lives. For them, that is the key to the real story of Kurozumi Munetada.

And now, Kurozumikyō takes satisfaction in making such knowledge available on a wider scale.

Previous Studies

Kurozumikyō and its founder have been studied by English-speaking scholars more than most Shinto denominations. The earliest substantial study is the work of Charles W. Hepner, placing the founder's life and teaching in context of Shinto history and supplying much detailed information. The best of an older generation's concern for objectivity and detailed information is seen in Hepner's work.[13]

Nobuhara Taisen, who is a philosopher living in the Okayama region, presents a philosopher's appreciation of Munetada as a spiritual figure. His work calls to a westerner's mind the nonchalant spirituality of St. Francis of Assisi; and indeed, this quality is visible in "Stories of the Founder" furnished in our present biography (Appendix).[14]

Helen Hardacre's close study of the life of a Kurozumi congregation, which included a survey of the founder's life, is our best introduction in English. Her study brought out Kurozumikyō as similar to other postwar religious movements in being based in traditional Japanese "core values."[15]

Our own book made a fresh contribution by presenting "insider" along with "outsider" materials. Three chapters by The Reverend Kurozumi Muneharu, two of them originally written for Kurozumikyō members, and translations of poetry of the founder, give a hitherto unavailable view of their teachings in action. The book was designed to help a reader with little background in study of Japan to appreciate what Kurozumi Shinto is about. What Kurozumi Munetada stood for, coming out of the broad tradition of pre-modern Japan as he did, is basic to Japanese national character. The narrowing impact of State Shinto, and the more recent amnesiac effects of Japanese peoples' concentration on economic development, are such that *The Opening Way* tells a story important to be heard.

How This Book Came into English

The Reverend Kurozumi Tadaaki is in key position to write this biography. For more than three decades he served in a number of key educational posts in Kurozumikyō headquarters. He also was the priest in charge of the Munetada Shrine in the Omoto section of Okayama that had until 1974 been the headquarters shrine. On the grounds is the house built for the Founder in 1848, still accessible as a museum housing artifacts of his life. Drawing on Kurozumi archives, on the Founder's letters and poetry, and on reports written by his immediate disciples, he weaves an account that establishes Munetada Kami as a spiritual authority and example worthy of respect from readers of today.

The Opening Way has gone through several stages in its progress toward this edition. An initial translation of the *Kyōsoden (Biography of the Founder)* by Kurozumi Tadaaki was prepared by Professor Harold Wright and Julie Iezzi. Wright, of Antioch College near my own institution, had already translated a selection of the Founder's poetry for *Kurozumi Shinto; an American Dialogue.* Subsequently, a parallel, more literal translation of the biography was provided by Kamiya Sumio, then a senior member of the staff of the Hayashibara Institute of Okayama. Taken together, the two versions gave me an invaluable parallax to the author's meaning.

The text went through four or five rounds of editing, with pages and chapters going back and forth over the Pacific, searching for the better word, the better phrase. The style is, I hope, sufficiently idiomatic, without losing the metaphors and viewpoint of the original, so as to supply a consistent "middle distance" empathetic to the author's thinking. Explanatory notes at many points suggest sources of further information and perspective. If the author, and through him Kurozumi Munetada of whom he speaks, has been enabled to "come nearer" the English reader whose experience and culture are rather different, my purpose will be fulfilled.

After work on *The Opening Way* was virtually complete, the author decided to add a selection of fourteen stories of the Founder as an appendix. These stories have an honored place in Kurozumi tradition, since, as the author indicates, the real canon for Kurozumikyō is not a book but the Founder himself. Retelling these stories is an immediate means to get close to him, and to know directly the force of his enlightened life.[16]

Acknowledgements and Thanks

Profound thanks are due to a number of people who helped me in addition to the principal translators. Professor Nishide Kimiyuke, Fulbright exchange professor at Wright State University, gave help at key points; Fujimoto Atsuko, David Stoesz, and my colleague Professor Kenji Oshiro provided assistance. The Hayashibara Institute of Okayama, through its president Hayashibara Ken, assisted enormously by making Kamiya Sumio available for extended periods of time. Thanks are due Anima Publications for permission to use poetry of the founder as published in *Kurozumi Shinto* (Anima Publications, 1989); changes from Harold Wright's version are all acknowledged. Most of all I thank the author, The Reverend Kurozumi Tadaaki, and The Reverend Kurozumi Muneharu, Sixth Patriarch of Kurozumikyō, for entrusting the task to me. For any errors that might have escaped our vigilance I take full responsibility.

Willis Stoesz
Emeritus Professor
Wright State University
Dayton, Ohio 45435

Fig. 1 The Reverend Kurozumi Muneharu is the Sixth Patriarch of Kurozumikyō, in direct succession and descent from the Founder. *Courtesy of Kurozumikyō.*

Foreword

The Reverend Kurozumi Muneharu
Chief Patriarch of Kurozumikyō

The path Kurozumi Munetada followed as Founder of Kurozumikyō can be briefly described as the way to become both fully human and fully divine (kami). He dedicated his life to enabling all to reach this goal, and to doing everything in his own life with utmost sincerity and singleheartedness.

When we reflect on the way he exerted sincerity toward everyone, we see that he always believed firmly that life is a place of training *(dōjō)* for cultivating and developing one's own heart. Already during his childhood his sincerity was visible in the way he showed filial piety to his parents. He found sacred significance in all of life, in all beings and in everything about him. This can be seen in his habit of giving prayerful thanks even to a worn-out pair of straw sandals before disposing of them. His prayer was that everyone would find the greatest possible meaning and worth in their lives, giving service in just such a spirit. He established a faith for all to follow in which all equally could do this, a religion that is a way of appreciating the value and vitality that the Great Kami has imparted to life.

This way of life, showing respect to our fellow humans and giving value to whatever we do, is essential to us today, living in a time when we are about to welcome in the twenty-first century. Munetada was fully conscious that in each of us resides the inner impulse of Great Kami, the divided portion *(bunshin)* of the Divine Heart accorded to each one of us. Throughout his life he expressed respect to the sacred Deity present in everyone, thus living his life in a bright spirit of harmony with all beings. I believe there is much we all can learn from how he lived his daily life.

It happens that this year is the twentieth anniversary of the move of the Headquarters of Kurozumikyō to its new location at Shintozan. The former headquarters at Omoto had served as the seat of our organization for over 160 years. We value the publication of *The Opening Way* as a significant way of commemorating this milestone.

We also remember with pleasure an international symposium held at Shintozan in 1990, the Shinto International Workshop on Global Survival and Peace sponsored by the Global Forum of Religious and Parliamentary Leaders on Human Survival. This followed their earlier conferences in Great Britain and in Moscow. It was the first international conference Kurozumikyō had sponsored. The members of the executive committee of the Forum gathered to study Shinto, the basis of the spirituality and way of thinking of the Japanese people, as they prepared for their international conference in Kyoto in 1993.

Gathered at Shintozan were believers and ministers of Christianity including the Russian Orthodox Church, Islam, Judaism, Hinduism, Confucianism, Buddhism, Shinto, and of Native American religion. Attending also were many prominent leaders from the fields of natural science, politics, business, industry, journalism and social welfare, totalling about 90 people from eleven countries. They took part in a four-day schedule that began each day with the traditional sunrise service of *Nippai,* our prayer to the rising sun. The conference concluded with a visit to the Ise Grand Shrine in Mie Prefecture, the central shrine of Shinto.

This workshop provided all who attended a new sense of the blessings we owe to nature and of the importance of maintaining the purity of our inner hearts. This indeed is the goal of the way of life that Munetada pursued, and that he fully expressed in his own personality.

We owe this careful publication of the English version of the *Kurozumikyō Kyōsoden* to the author, The Reverend Kurozumi Tadaaki, Vice Patriarch of Kurozumikyō; to Professor Willis Stoesz of Wright State University, Editor; to Professor Harold Wright and Julie Iezzi, translators; to Professor Helen Hardacre, Harvard University, who first pointed out the need for an English version; to Mr. Kamiya Sumio of Okayama, an admirer of Kurozumikyō's many contributions to international service and friendship, who assisted in innumerable ways; to Professor Nishide Kimiyuki of Mie University, member of a Kurozumikyō family who furnished valuable help to Professor Stoesz in understanding the original book. I express to them all my sincere and heartfelt gratitude for their generous contributions.

I hope that readers of *The Opening Way* in the English-speaking world will find the book helpful as they seek ways to improve their lives and to help those dear to them find answers to the question of how best to live life today.

On the first day of the commemorative twentieth anniversary year of establishing Shintozan.

Kurozumi Muneharu,
Chief Patriarch

Fig. 2 The Reverend Kurozumi Tadaaki, Author, is the Vice Patriarch of Kurozumikyō. The photo is taken on the veranda of the Main Shrine *(Daikyōden)*. *Courtesy of Kurozumikyō.*

Introduction

Several years after my return to Kurozumikyō Headquarters in 1949, I wrote "The Biography of the Founder of Kurozumikyō" as a series in *Nisshin,* the monthly journal published by Headquarters and distributed to the followers. I did so at the request of its editors. Later the series was compiled into a book and published by the Secretariat of the Young People's Kurozumikyō Association.

Only one edition was published because I felt I had been presumptuous, and repented of that. So, I allowed it to go out of print. During the following years, however, I received repeated requests and suggestions to republish it. I agreed that a revised biography of our Founder was needed, but my busy daily work prevented my undertaking the assignment.

Then, some years ago, the distinguished leaders of Kurozumikyō Headquarters approached me and explained that they believe the Founder's biography is indispensable to the younger generations. It would enable them to understand the basic teachings of Kurozumikyō and to carry on the faith. I felt that merely republishing the original would be inappropriate and unforgivable. I would have to write a new version to meet this need. This is the background of my decision to write this biography all over again.

When we look around us it is easy to see that everybody has his or her own idea about how to live. We can also see that being confronted in the course of life with hardship and anguish in varying measure is common to us all. Some are crushed by these experiences and become grief stricken, thinking that this is just how life is, facing it as a painful and bitter fate. Many grow tired of it all and give up on life, becoming angry and blaming others. The number of those who grow weary of the world and lose hope in life seems countless.

The Founder of Kurozumikyō is one to whom we can turn when we suffer such experiences. In 1812 when he was 33 years old, he unfortunately lost both of his parents within a week. He had been outstandingly dutiful and obedient to them. In his very great grief and sorrow he contracted pulmonary tuberculosis. There was no effective therapy for tuberculosis at this time, over 150 years ago, and the disease was regarded as hopeless and fatal. But, after being bedridden for more than a year, he suddenly experienced a flash of hope amidst his hours of sadness and gloom. He saw the light of grace emanating from Amaterasu Ōmikami, revealing her Divine Way.

Thanks to this experience the Founder escaped death. Not only did he recover from his illness, but he discovered the Great Way as the means of liberating himself, and us as well, from all the anguish and suffering we experience. His discovery showed him how to deal with the ordinary aspects of daily life as well as with its difficulties. Munetada regarded this healing experience as Amaterasu Ōmikami directly entrusting him with the Divine Mission to propagate her Great Way. Kurozumikyō followers revere this event as the Direct Bestowal of the Divine Mission. For the rest of his life, more than 30 years, the Founder devoted himself to this mandate. He diligently pursued missionary work in propagating the Way, offering his help to invalids and to those in despair.

It is our duty always to praise the sacred life and teachings of our Founder Kurozumi Munetada. He is the guide who leads us through our life's course. He sheds light on our path to give us hope. Through respecting his personality and studying his personal history and achievements we come to learn his holy teachings, which show us how to cope with the many events we face each day in life, including its many adversities and diseases.

Morishita Keitan (1824-1891), who was appointed the Secretary General of Kurozumikyō Headquarters on his retirement from government service, started his life as a low-level foot soldier of the Okayama clan, but diligence helped him attain high office as the Governor of Oita Prefecture in Kyushu. We are told that in his later years he said that in military and political matters he always followed the Founder's teachings, and this enabled him always to do what was right and to stay free of mistakes. I am confident that you will find this perception still holds true today. The singular religious devotion the Founder observed throughout his life makes a great impression on us as well. We too find it instructive and inspiring.

The characteristic of Kurozumikyō that most clearly distinguishes it from other religions is the fact that its doctrine and creed consist of the life, personality, thoughts, and ideas of the Founder. The doctrine of Kurozumikyō is neither a comprehensive compilation of ideas and thoughts of different Shinto sects or of Confucianism, nor is it a doctrine prepared and compiled by leading disciples. It is not any sort of theoretical compilation. Its beginnings are in the hereditary folk belief of Shinto that was observed by the Japanese in their daily lives from the early days of our history. Kurozumikyō developed out of this traditional Shinto through the unique and spectacular religious experience of the Founder. The Direct Bestowal of Divine Mission on him in 1814, which established that experience, is the basis of this new and singular form of religious faith.

Kurozumikyō is not a teaching of lip service or of honeyed words. It is a teaching that was actually attained by the personal experiences, ideas, and thoughts of this single individual. In other words, the teaching consists only of the personal achievement of a real person, the Founder. He seems to extend his hands to us, telling us to follow the footprints he has left for us. Kurozumikyō members regard him as a pathfinder. The term we use, *misebumi,* refers to one who, in days when there were few bridges over rivers, would wade a stream to test the depth and flow of the water to find the safest and surest way to cross over.

Tracing the steps the divine pathfinder left for us is a matter of practice and action. When we study the personal history of the Founder and think deeply about it we are already beginning to follow that practice. This is what the doctrine of Kurozumikyō is all about.

The life of the Founder can without exaggeration be summed up as concerned with fulfilling filial duties. Indeed, he was born to fulfill his filial duties to his parents, he became ill because of his anguish in losing his parents, and he attained his spiritual awakening through pursuing his filial duties. It was the strong sense of filial duty he had felt from his very young days that threw him into such a Slough of Despond, bedridden with an incurable disease.

Then, when he was very close to dying, he realized the importance of shifting his filial affection for his parents to a filial piety devoted to Amaterasu Ōmikami, the Kami who governs and oversees all of Heaven and Earth. As a result, the Founder discovered how to combine this affection for his parents with religious faith, thus producing a better form of filial piety. In one of his letters *(Gobun)* he wrote:

> To leave everything to Amaterasu Ōmikami is like having the same heart a child has in obeying its parents' instruction. Faith in Kami is just the same as filial affection. My own religious practice *(shugyō)*, and what I teach to others, consists in following the divine words of Kami, the inner biddings of Heaven, in just that spirit. Since all that we do is the result of what happens within the divine heart of Kami, there is no chance of going wrong. So, there is no room for any kind of fear or anxiety. If we lead our daily lives leaving all to the guidance of Heaven's inner mind, we will be sure to receive the instruction we need easily and directly, whatever the matter may be. When we live in this receptive spirit, life is nothing but joy.
>
> *Gobun* 19

Since Amaterasu Ōmikami, the Mother Kami who creates and oversees all beings in Heaven and on Earth, is our true parent, we should carry everything in our daily lives to her. We should be assured and have absolutely no anxieties that the Kami of Creation will take care of our worries and lead us through all hardships. This is just the way parents dedicate themselves, working hard for the interest of their children when they suffer trouble or are in distress and misfortune. They will even sacrifice themselves for their children's benefit. In the same way, leading our daily lives in response to the will of Amaterasu Ōmikami can never be a mistake.

Whatever the event or circumstance, throughout his whole life Munetada did everything as Amaterasu Ōmikami directly ordered him. Munetada looked at his life in a positive way, always obedient to her will. The doctrine of the Founder may be described as teaching us how we also may receive the Divine Mission from Amaterasu Ōmikami. We learn from him how to live our lives consistently with the decree of Heaven, the Great Way. If we live consistently with the Great Way, our life will be a cheerful and happy one. As we see from the letter quoted above, the Founder spent his life in great spiritual peace and enlightenment and in comfort and ease.

It is my earnest desire that readers will comprehend the importance of our following the pathfinder, and of joining our efforts to help create a brighter society and community, so that we may lead our lives cheerfully and happily and with meaning.

July, 1974
Kurozumi Tadaaki

Note on the English Edition

This publication of *Kurozumikyō Kyōsoden (Biography of the Founder of Kurozumikyō)* is a great satisfaction to me and my personal honor. I owe my sincerest thanks to the deep comprehension and generous cooperation of many, including Professor Willis Stoesz of Wright State University in Dayton, Ohio, U.S.A.

The original book is the fruit of some forty years of study and research in the stories and records of Kurozumi Munetada, the Founder of Kurozumikyō, whom I hold in the highest esteem and reverence. These materials have been thoughtfully and carefully handed down to us by our predecessors in writing and by word of mouth.

Nothing can give me greater pleasure than the fact that the eyes of people in the English-speaking world now have easy access to this biography, originally published only in Japanese and available only here.

No other joy can surpass knowing that wide recognition can now be given that such outstanding people lived in this corner of the Orient, particularly here in Okayama, Japan. I am very glad that a wider circle of readers may now be served by this guidance and assistance for the living of their lives, enabling them to enjoy life's fulfillment.

On the Eighth Day of the
Third Month, 1993
(My Seventy-Fourth Birthday)
Kurozumi Tadaaki

Fig. 3 The present main shrine *(Daikyōden)* at Shintozan, at the near southwest of Okayama. It was completed and consecrated in 1974. *Courtesy of Kurozumikyō.*

Chapter One

Birth

Family and Lineage

Kurozumi Munetada (1780-1850), founder of Kurozumikyō, was born toward the end of the Edo period (1600-1868) on the 26th day of the 11th month of 1780. According to the calendar then in use, this was the day of the winter solstice.[17] The place was the hamlet of Kaminakano (or simply "Nakano") near the village of Imamura in Mino county in the province of Bizen. Today Kaminakano is a part of the city of Okayama, and Bizen is part of Okayama Prefecture. His father, Kurozumi Muneshige, served in this place as priest of the Imamura Shrine. His mother's name was Tsuta. Munetada was the couple's third son.

The Kurozumi family at one time served as samurai to the Southern Court during the age of the Northern and Southern Courts (1336-1392),[18] but after the two courts were united, the Kurozumis gave up their work as samurai and moved to Bizen. Here they began service as Shinto priests at the Sansha-gu (Sansha Shrine), so named because three shrines had been combined into one.

The samurai heritage is an important part of Kurozumi family tradition. In later years, the family used to hold a ceremony in memory of this heritage each year on the eleventh day of the first month, even up to the beginning of the Meiji period. At this armor celebration ceremony the Kurozumi armor was placed in the household alcove (*tokonoma*) while the ancestors were remembered with praise. The head of the family would urge the current generation to revere their ancestors, and afterwards all those attending would join together in a ceremonial feast. Even today the ancestral armor is preserved and cherished as a Kurozumi family treasure.

The Kurozumi family moved to Okayama around the time Ukita Naoie had brought the entire Bizen area under his control, with his headquarters castle in the Numa area inside present-day Okayama City. Soon after that (1575), he built Okayama castle as his new headquarters. He built it on the site of the Sansha-gu, where the Kurozumi family was serving, and so the kami of the shrine were re-enshrined in nearby Imamura. So as to remain in service, the Kurozumis accompanied the move and relocated there.

The village of Imamura already had a shrine, called Imamura Hachiman-gu.[19] With the moving of Sansha Shrine to Imamura, the kami of both places were combined and the shrine was renamed Sansha Hachiman-gu. Later it came to be known simply as Imamura-gu, and it was here that the Kurozumis served for generations as Shinto priests.

Most records of their early history have been lost and many details are unknown, but it is certain that sometime during the Genroku period (1688-1703) a person named Kurozumi Muneyoshi was in service at Imamura Shrine. He was followed by Munenobu, Muneshige, Munechika, and then Muneshige (1741-1812), the father of Munetada, the Founder of Kurozumikyō.

Permission to serve as Shinto priests in most provinces of Japan, including the Bizen area, was under the authority of the Yoshida family in Kyoto during this period. This was true also of the Sansha Shrine and led to their appointing the Kurozumi family to its service. The appointment was to the position of *negi* so that, in common with other Shinto priests who had this title, they had the power to delegate priestly duties. The letters of authorization to Muneyoshi and to his successors are still preserved today.

Muneshige, the Founder's father, was a gentle, devoted, and much admired priest. He married Tsuta, the fourth daughter of Nagase Naomasa, the chief priest of Shirahige Shrine not far away. Together they had three boys and one girl. The eldest son, Inosuke, was taken at a young age into the Kirino family to become their adopted heir, but passed away in 1823. The Kirinos were the same family into which Nagase Naomasa's fifth daughter, Kane, had married. The next child of the Kurozumis, a daughter named Kuma, also married into this family.

Their second son, Iheiji, having studied swordsmanship from a young age, decided to leave Bizen and try to establish himself as a swordsman in the city of Edo where the Tokugawa Shoguns had their headquarters and from where they ruled Japan. However, he died there in 1804 at the age of 29.

It was due to these family circumstances that the Founder, Munetada, though born the youngest, moved into position to carry on the family line. The families of Shinto priests in the Bizen domain *(han)* were of samurai class and possessed rather high status, being given the rank of *kachi*.[20] They by no means ranked low economically or socially, and generally were well-regarded community leaders.

The Founder's birth occurred on the day, month, and year of the Rat. In the Chinese calendar, the Rat is the first in the cycle of twelve symbols, signifying beginnings, and from ancient times it has been considered auspicious. Moreover, his birth also came on the winter solstice, which in the midst of cold winter tells us that spring is not far away. All this makes the day of his birth a most auspicious one indeed.

The exact place of his birth is believed to be where the sanctuary of the Munetada Shrine now stands.[21] When he was born his father was 40 and his mother 37, and it appears that the maturity of both his parents had a great effect on the Founder's formative years.

Until 1794, when at the age of 15 the rite marking his attainment of manhood was observed, the Founder was known by his childhood name of Gonkichi. Then he was renamed Sanokichi. Then, when in 1804 he became the official head of the family at age 25, he changed his name to Ugenji. Finally, when he assumed the priestly rank of *negi*[22] of Imamura Shrine in 1824, he took the name Sakyo Munetada. He was then 45 years old by Japanese reckoning.

Fig. 4   The Founder's Birth House. In former days, upperclass families had birthing houses separate from their residences, in accord with traditional belief in the ritual impurity of the birth process. *Courtesy of Kurozumikyō.*

Historical Background

The Founder lived during the mid-to-late Edo period. The emperor reigning at the time was Kokaku (r. 1780-1817), and the shogun was Tokugawa Ieharu, the tenth in the line of Tokugawa shoguns.. During the early part of this period Tanuma Okitsugu, the councillor to the shogun, controlled the country and it was a time of rampant corruption.[23] Though a firm, stable feudal system still maintained order in society, cries from the intelligentsia were beginning to be heard, pointing to contradictions in the social system and calling for greater respect for human life and dignity.

In Bizen it was a somewhat different story. The enlightened administration of the Ikeda clan during the whole Tokugawa period provided a more favorable public climate than in the country generally. The head of the clan at this time was Ikeda Harumasa, but the basic structure of the government had for the most part been set up during the time of the clan's founder, the *daimyō* Mitsumasa.[24]

Lord Mitsumasa (1609-1682) was already in his own times highly praised by his subjects and by people elsewhere as a wise ruler. He promoted the development of his domain with the welfare and prosperity of his subjects in mind. He encouraged industries, sponsored projects in land reclamation and construction of irrigation canals, and promoted education. His benevolent attitude set the tone of the policy the Ikeda clan followed in succeeding generations. Visible evidence of it today is the famous Shizutani School in Bizen, the first school in Japan that was open to commoners. The buildings are still in excellent condition and are often visited by tourists.

Here we will take note only of some aspects of Mitsumasa's rule that relate to his administration of religion. Mitsumasa revered Confucianism highly and wished to combine its doctrines with those of Shinto, forming a unification of the two. At the same time, he was severely critical of Buddhism. Taking quite a grim stance in his attitude towards Buddhist temples and monks, he worked actively to reduce their numbers. Many monks were expelled and forced to return to secular life, where they were carefully assisted in finding new occupations. Later, when Mitsumasa's son, Tsunamasa, succeeded to his father's position, some of these vacated temples were allowed to resume their earlier religious activities.

In his time, however, Mitsumasa not only carefully regulated the Buddhist temples but also the many private, unauthorized shrines. He tore down over 10,000 such shrines *(inshi)*, mostly devoted to spirits the people feared and worshiped only to avoid their negative influence. Those deities he considered to be of value were gathered at newly-built shrines, generally referred to as *yosemiya*.

His goal in this effort was to promote whatever encouraged good conduct among his subjects, based on honesty and justice and following his principle of never failing to reward meritorious service nor letting a fault go unpunished. After his reforms the total number of shrines left in his domain, those with well-supported lineages or with historical significance, was about 600.

Mitsumasa also greatly encouraged academic studies. He is reported to have established a school in every district in his territory. He was concerned to establish the Confucian political ideals of sincerity and humanity so as to rule the country well and to treat his subjects with virtue, moral excellence, and benevolence. He actively fostered a sense of filial piety among the youth of his domain. Because of his outstanding administration and his excellent choice of capable people to serve in all branches of his government, education increasingly flourished in his realm. This attitude toward the social and political environment was passed on to his successors, and was inherited by Ikeda Harumasa who governed Bizen when Munetada was born.

Thus, while the Bizen area in which Munetada lived shared in the troubles that affected Japanese people generally during the late Edo period, it had, during the time he was growing up, a public climate concerned with high ideals of the common life because of its Ikeda heritage.

Chapter Two

Setting His Life's Goals

His Childhood

Honest by nature, faithful to the Kami of the Sun, and obedient to his parents.

This is the way our Founder Munetada is described in the words of the disciple Hoshijima Ryōhei (1835-1879) in his work *Short Biography of our Founder Munetada.* He is similarly described by Kawakami Chūsho (1795-1862) in his *Biography of the Great Deity:*[25]

Our late Teacher had a heart of great honesty and compassion. He quickly and naturally understood others' griefs and sorrows. He piously did his duty to his parents, and was most sincerely attentive to all people with whom he had relationship. He was very strict in everything he did and serious in his thinking.

From this we can see something of the honest and dutiful nature for which he was known in his community. When young he was commended as "the filial child of Nakano."

There are a number of stories about him that reflect his obedience to his parents from a very early age. One took place when he was seven. One day, after it had been raining, he was going out to play. As he was leaving the house he heard his father calling after him saying, "The roads are still muddy so you had better wear your *geta* [wooden clogs]," to which he replied with an obedient "Yes." The mother, however, not knowing about the father's instructions, also called out after her son, "The streets are all dry now so it will be all right to wear *zori* [sandals]." The two completely different instructions left the young Munetada in a dilemma. After thinking it over for a while he solved it by leaving the house wearing a *geta* on one foot and a *zori* on the other. Faced by his parents with a perplexing situation, in his childlike way of thinking he obeyed them both by wearing one of each of the two assigned footwear (*Tales of the Founder* 14).[26]

When Gonkichi was a little older, about 12 or 13, he overheard some neighbors saying that his father was looking noticeably older. Hearing this, young Munetada began going to a stream to perform cold water ablutions early every morning in hopes of bringing longevity to his parents, and offering daily prayers at the Imamura Shrine in their behalf (*Tales of the Founder* 15).

Around this time there was in the area of Kaminakano a private school where children were taught calligraphy.[27] Gonkichi also attended this school and studied calligraphy under one Mr. Hanafusa, the instructor. On one occasion the teacher was missing some money that he felt certain he had left in the drawer of his desk. Hoping to get a confession from a guilty student, he questioned the whole class, threatening to keep them all after school. One student, he noticed, turned a little pale. The teacher naturally began to wonder if this one had taken the money, though from the boy's everyday conduct it was most unthinkable that he would have done such a thing.

However, some days later while going about some other business the teacher happened to open a small drawer in a chest, where he unexpectedly found the money he had thought was stolen. Thinking about it, he soon realized he had mislaid the money there himself. He immediately called before him the child he had suspected and asked why he had looked so upset on the day of the questioning. The boy replied:

> Sir, when you said that we couldn't go home I thought it would be awful. You see, when it is time for me to come home from school, my mother goes out to the gate of our house to wait for me. If I were going to be late I knew she would certainly be worried. So, not knowing what to do, I suppose I did look upset. Sir, I am really sorry.

Upon receiving such an apology, the teacher, embarrassed by his own actions, realized that he was not fit to be the teacher of such a child. He introduced him to a man named Ichimura Sanzo, a teacher of young children who also served as a private secretary to the ruling Ikeda family. This child was, of course, Gonkichi, the young Munetada. From that time on he studied at the Ichimura school along with children of samurai families. Here he was not only taught calligraphy but also given an introduction to the Chinese classics.

At the Ichimura school Gonkichi again was punctual in his attendance. During the mornings he studied seriously and had the composure of an adult, even though he was still quite young. Yet, towards evening when the time was nearing to return home, he became unaccountably restless and fidgety. Mr. Ichimura, thinking this behavior a little strange, questioned him about it. He replied:

> Sir, you see, my mother stands by the gate waiting for me to come home. She worries if I am even a little late, so I really like to get home as quickly as I can.

Mr. Ichimura was as deeply impressed with the sincere filial affection of the child toward his parents as his previous teacher had been (*Tales of the Founder* 16).

Encouraged to study calligraphy and the Chinese classics at the Ichimura school, Gonkichi in the end became a polished calligrapher of rare talent. Moreover, his aptitude for the Chinese classics had much to do with the life goals he later set for himself.

His Adolescence

The young Munetada entered adolescence with the new name Sanokichi. As the range of his activities and concerns widened, his knowledge of his surroundings also was broadened, and he saw from his own experience the daily troubles we all confront. He saw for himself the world's anxieties, contradictions, pain, sickness, poverty, quarrels, and conflicts, things of which he had been unaware when younger.

When he was 16 or 17 the Ikeda clan sponsored a grand hunt of wild boar and deer, and Sanokichi went with a friend to watch. The event was intended as a display and promotion of martial accomplishments. Before the occasion was half over, however, Sanokichi suddenly left. Later he explained, "I can't stand watching the sight of taking a life, even the life of an animal. It is unbearably heartless" (*Tales of the Founder* 17).

During this time Sanokichi grew even stronger in his feelings of filial piety towards his parents. It was not only that he didn't want to cause them any anxiety, nor that he simply always obeyed them. The young man wanted to bring them real joy in life and it was for their sake that he began to think about becoming a well-known and deeply respected person in society.

Clearly, his wishes in this direction were strongly influenced by his study of Chinese classics at the Ichimura school, especially *The Classic of Filial Piety*. But at the same time, he certainly was influenced also by seeing the disasters and suffering happening in those times. No doubt Sanokichi felt deeply that becoming a perfected and wise personality, a kami-like person, would enable him to offer a way of salvation to people suffering from hardships.

Setting His Life's Goal

In his sincere pondering about becoming a kami,²⁸ he began to read a great many books and to question his elders. But satisfactory answers to his questions were not forthcoming. Yet he did not weaken in his resolve to reach this purified and divine status and by this means become able to aid the many suffering people of the world. He felt that by dedicating his life to this service he would ultimately achieve the highest possible expression of filial piety. Night and day for months, even years, he thought of little else. He must attain his goal, nothing else would do.

He was certain that people naturally possess something we may call "conscience." This is an inner bidding of Heaven, so that everyone has the innate ability to tell the difference between good and evil, right and wrong.²⁹ Such a heart has been given us by Kami, a kami-heart. When we listen to Kami by means of this heart we can do only good. We can do no evil. Consequently, if we do listen to our conscience and do only good we can become one with Kami; indeed, we can become a living kami *(ikigami)*. Of this he had no doubt.

Thus, with this kind of strong belief, he firmly set for himself the goal of becoming a living kami. He was twenty years old at the time.

As he worked toward this goal he reflected on every single thing that he did. If he felt in his heart that some action was a bad thing to do, he strove hard never to do it. Since he was a good person with excellent qualities, naturally humble, extremely reverent, and deeply dutiful towards his parents, he was able to make progress in his religious practice.

Soon after starting in this way he made up a list of Five Articles by which he would guide himself in his daily activities. These Articles, or Principles, closely supported his effort. We can see that they clearly spell out what sort of things one can within one's heart know to be bad.

The original form of the Five Articles is:

Five Rules to be Followed at Home

1. Born into a family deeply following the faith, I pledge never to be without faith.
2. I pledge not to be filled with self-conceit nor look down upon others.
3. I pledge not to increase the evil of my own heart by focusing on the evil of others.
4. I pledge not to be negligent in attending my family occupation unless I am ill.
5. Since I have entered the Way of Sincerity, I pledge that my heart shall never be allowed to lack sincerity.

> Standing before me
>> others hold up mirrors
>>> as their own hearts
> And there within I can see
>> my heart being reflected.

The above articles are awesome. I shall follow them as principles of my religious discipline.

The original copy of these Five Articles is now preserved and on view at the Marukoto Center, a conference building which is part of Kurozumikyō headquarters at Shintozan near Okayama. The paper on which they were written is now soot-covered and faded, but it was originally hung by the young Munetada on the wall of his study where he could see the Articles daily as instructions to himself.

All in all, the goal Munetada set for himself in life is extraordinarily ambitious, setting forth a new human ideal as it does. Yet, at the time Munetada practiced them unpretentiously and tirelessly as an ongoing religious discipline. He never lost sight of their radiant and original importance.

Munetada's later Direct Bestowal of Divine Mission is considered to be his Great Awakening. By comparison, setting his goal should be considered a "lesser awakening." However, his great purpose, coming to fulfillment twelve or thirteen years after first setting forth in this way, glowed brilliantly within his harmonious personality.

After Setting His Life's Goals

Along with this, the remarkable influence of what he learned in his home must also be considered. Kurozumi Munetada was born to two fine parents in a harmonious middle class family which had held religious convictions for generation after generation. From the time of his childhood he studied calligraphy and came to be known in the countryside where he lived as a most talented calligrapher. He even gave lessons to children of the area. Also, since he was quite skilled in chanting Noh texts, we can assume to some accurate degree what sort of person he was.[30]

In the spring of 1803 he went on a pilgrimage to the Grand Shrines of Ise,[31] something he had wanted to do for a long time. A distant journey of over a month, it wasn't an easy task. Not everyone could do it. However, his desire to make this trip must be seen in relation to the goal he had set for himself. Amaterasu Ōmikami, the Sun Kami herself, was enshrined at Ise, and this place played a central role in his developing faith. The *Chronology of Kurozumi Documents*[32] records that Munetada's father, Muneshige, entered his name in the petition log authorizing such pilgrimages, indicating his parental support.

In the following year, Iheiji, the second of his brothers, died in the distant city of Edo at the age of 29. This was the brother who had left home to study swordsmanship. As the elder of the two remaining brothers after the first son entered another family through adoption, Iheiji felt an obligation to succeed to the household headship though he had left his family. Not long after he went to Edo, he had sent some ancient Shinto scrolls to his younger brother, an excellent gift for the pious young man. In this way he expressed his gratitude to his younger brother for taking care of the family in his place. Still, Munetada felt that he had to increase his own feelings of filial piety to make up for those lacking in his brother. He was aided greatly in this effort by his ever-deepening devotion to the kami whom he served as a Shinto priest.

It was because of his remaining brother's death that Munetada was designated as heir to the family headship, though born as the third son. He was renamed Ugenji to reflect his change in status. He was 25 years old.

Marriage

His marriage seems to have taken place in the early spring of 1806. He married a woman by the name of Iku (1785-1848) from the nearby village of Fukushima. It is said that Iku had been walking barefoot every morning from her home in Fukushima to worship in Imamura, as a prayer for the recovery of her foster father who was sick. This act of devotion caught the attention of another Shinto priest named Karube Ukyo, who served as go-between to bring about the marriage. Munetada also was probably much impressed to find a young woman with such feelings of faith and filial piety that she would walk over five kilometers every morning as an act of worship. He probably also believed that if he were to marry such a wife she would certainly be most dutiful towards his own parents also.

Munetada was not disappointed. Gentle in disposition, she did care for his parents with the deep devotion he had hoped for. It is well-known, too, that she was a most supportive wife to her husband during the course of their marriage. It could be said that Iku later on was, in a very practical sense, Munetada's first disciple. She was always at his side listening to his teachings. She heard his sermons at home, of course, but she also accompanied him on his journeys. She received all visitors who came to worship from places both near and far with deep warmth. Her contributions were referred to as "sermonless sermons" and "silent leadership," and they were many.

Not much information concerning Iku is available but it is known that she was always a power behind the scenes and that she accomplished much. There are traces of her in the Kurozumi teachings. It was well understood that she was an important influence, as his wife, upon the Founder and his work.

On the tenth day of the second month of 1807, the first daughter was born to Iku and Munetada. However, their application for permission to marry was not presented until the eighth month of 1811. The reason for this discrepancy is the custom in those days of waiting for the father to retire before making the proper application. It was considered important first to arrange for formal succession to family headship, and this was done with the retirement of Munetada's father in 1810.

Anyway, Munetada's parents, after the marriage, enjoyed excellent health as they were so affectionately cared for by the young couple. And now with a child joining them, this harmonious household in its peace and happiness was the envy of many. Then, too, Munetada, building on the goals he had set for himself in his early 20's, made steady progress in his religious development. He was steadily approaching his time of fulfillment. He was soon to attain complete comprehension *(satori)*.[33]

In life, however, light is often followed by shadows; or, as it is sometimes said, fortune and misfortune are as closely interwoven as the alternate strands of a rope. In the midst of contentment the unhappy and the unexpected thing can occur. Munetada, who was nearing the summit of happiness, had an unexpected storm blow into his life. Nothing worse could have happened. His parents died in rapid succession.

Chapter Three

Direct Bestowal of Divine Mission

The Death of His Parents

In the autumn of 1812 dysentery attacked the province of Bizen like an evil spirit. It took away both of Munetada's parents in a short span of time. His mother, after only a brief period of illness with high fever and diarrhea, passed away during the night of the 29th day of the eighth month. Soon after, as if in pursuit, his father passed away on the fifth day of the ninth month. Tsuta, his mother, was 69. Muneshige was 72.

Munetada and his wife had devoted all the energy they could to the care and nursing of his parents, who in the end left this world quite fulfilled. Nevertheless, to Munetada, who was 33 at the time and had since childhood been far above average in his devotion to his parents, the sadness of having both his parents taken away within such a brief period as seven days was more than he could grasp.

The very purpose of his life had been taken away. He had centered his life goals, his religious practices, his marriage, indeed everything, around his filial piety. Now, he had lost everything worth living for.

Each day he would make countless visits to his parents' grave. One day, overcome with grief, he even fainted in the cemetery. He would secretly take out his parents' clothing to remind himself of them and of happier times through the lingering fragrance. Or, leaning against the rain shutters of the house, he would stare off into the sky blankly, unable to do anything. His days were spent in anguish until finally, in the fall of the following year, he took to his sickbed. He had pulmonary tuberculosis.

He remained in his sickbed for the rest of that year (1813) and even into the next. The middle of this New Year season (1814) brought a turn for the worse and he finally lapsed into a state so critical that there no longer seemed to be any hope of recovery. His illness, continuing during three calendar years, reached the point where it was thought that Munetada, totally incurable, would pass away at the age of 35.

The Enlightenment of His Heart

The 19th day of the first month of 1814 is remembered as the day he reached a state so critical that those close to him thought the end surely was near. The neighbors, who had such high regard for him, prayed for his recovery. Even so, his attending physician, Dr. Urata Shōzen, the doctor who was in service at the time to the ruling family of Bizen, diagnosed his condition as beyond hope. Munetada's childhood friend, Ono Saburobei, consulted a local fortune-teller, but he also pronounced that it was the divine will and nothing could be done about it. Munetada prepared himself for his approaching death.

Waiting calmly, he made a vow that after dying he would become a kami, one who would help the people of this earth and cure their illnesses.[34] In a final farewell to this world, he prayed to the sun, the kami of heaven and earth, and all the kami of the universe, following this with prayers to his ancestors and his parents. He thanked them for his life and for all the favors they had bestowed on him in his lifetime. His heart was then at rest. He had those nursing him move him closer to the veranda where he could see the sun, so that he could give his last sunrise prayer *(nippai)*.

At the moment he was prepared for death, having no regrets, his heart felt strangely at peace. As he then quietly reflected on the past, he thought:

> It was originally because of my grief at my parents' death that I became depressed and brought injury to my heart. That is why I am now in this incurable condition. My condition gradually got worse right up to the present moment. It has been a year and a half since my mother and father passed away, and my devotion to them has led me to drown in my sorrow, not thinking about the pain and suffering I brought on the body my parents have bequeathed me. How would my father and my mother feel to see me in this plight? They would certainly be saddened. What great grief it would be to them! Ah, I have been deeply mistaken. What a blunder I have committed! There is no excuse for it.
>
> Now, I don't have much longer to live. There is nothing I can do about that. But at least, for as long as I still have the breath of life in me, I will do what I can to make my parents happy. Since it was sadness and gloom which caused me to become ill, I must have a change of heart and become joyful and bright. At least if I use my last breaths to bring joy to my inner heart it will be an act of true filial piety. There is no doubt that my parents would be pleased.

In this way and at that moment, as his heart became clearer, Munetada moved toward his experience of bestowal of mission.

Until that time, in his long illness, he had been malcontent and dissatisfied. But now when he really thought about it, he saw that the loving care he received from his wife and daughter and the warm inquiries into his health and concern from relatives and neighbors were all things to be truly grateful for. His attitude toward them changed as in his heart he became aware that he owed all of it to the Divine Favor.

Then he felt a fresh concern, causing fresh distress. "If I were to die, what on earth would happen to my wife and daughter?" But then he realized that "my wife and daughter are both children of Heaven, sent down from Heaven, and would, without doubt, continue to be well in this life. Furthermore, I must be thankful for having such a fine wife and child."

Focusing his heart on these feelings of gratitude for the blessings of Heaven was Munetada's miraculous turning point. It was at this moment that he began to feel relief from his illness. It seemed as if the heaviness of his heart had been cleared away. Becoming more and more aware of a sense of gratitude for divine gifts, feelings of thankfulness welled up in his heart. This event is known as the First *Gohai*, or Sacred Experience of *Nippai*.[19]

His Complete Recovery

Sunset came on the day he was expected to die, as did night and the following dawn, but still death had not come. Up to this point, probably not even Munetada himself thought that recovery was possible. Yet with the passing of time, his condition continued to improve with each breath that he took as he came to know both mornings and evenings filled with the glow of joy. He was reborn out of the world of darkness in which he had been living, full of sorrow, into a bright world overflowing with joy and gratitude.

The *Short Biography* records:

In everything he saw, everything he heard, he came to feel gratitude for the blessings of heaven. By earnestly nurturing his heart by means of his own heart, his health also improved, as though he had been covered with wrappings of paper that were now being stripped from him, layer after thin layer, one at a time.

A heart which is always bright, vital, full of joy, wonder, and gratitude is, indeed, a heart as it was originally given us by Kami. But owing to various everyday troubles and hardships, we lose sight of it and choose a path of unhappiness. What again brings joy, wonder, and gratitude to us is our hearts themselves. This is the meaning of the expression "Nurturing our hearts by means of our own hearts."

Day after day, step by step, he gradually moved along the road to recovery until the 19th day of the third month. Then, though still in his sickbed, Munetada suddenly proposed to do the service of sunrise worship. Moreover, he wished this time to have a bath first. His wife quite firmly forbade him to do it; though on the road to recovery, his body was still severely weakened.

Usually, when his wife put a stop to something he went along with what she said and didn't do it. But this time he insisted so strongly that Iku finally called Ono Eizaburō, the village head, and his old childhood friend Ono Saburobei, for assistance and advice. Together they listened to Munetada's reasons for the request and, rather than trying to stop him, went along with the idea. They recognized Munetada as someone unusually great. Under normal circumstances he should have died in the first month of the year, but by some miracle, he had quite revived. He was not only still living but on the way to recovery. They could see, this was beyond the scale of ordinary men. If he wanted to do *nippai* in this way he should certainly be allowed to do it.

So in this way Munetada worshiped the sun as he had wished. It was a *nippai* full of deep gratitude and emotion. This day marked the end of over a year of sickness. It was a complete recovery.

It is described this way in the *Short Biography:*

> One day he left his sickbed, took a hot bath, and worshiped the sun. Thereupon his long illness vanished like the morning frost and he was at once completely healed.

This is referred to as his Second *Gohai.*

It was after the first *Gohai* that Munetada had come to understand that his illness occurred because his original heart had become melancholy, and that he only needed a cheerful, optimistic attitude to cure his illness. It was through the second *Gohai* that his belief came to be realized. He had received confirmation that Kami would always extend her help, and it was a powerful experience for him.

The Third Gohai: Direct Bestowal of Divine Mission

It was on the morning of the day of the winter solstice in the 11th month in 1814 as he performed *nippai* that his full revelation occurred. He was 35 years old. He later recalled his experience this way, as recorded in the *Gokōden:*[36]

The day of the winter solstice, a splendid and auspicious day when nature passes through seasonal changes, is also the day of my own birth. Having a birthday on the day of winter solstice is fortunate, but this year (1814) was very special with my having experienced the revival of my life by the blessing of Kami. This is indeed an incomparably auspicious birthday for which I am most grateful.

The *nippai* of that day was carried out with special care and deepest gratitude. With complete earnestness I respectfully offered up my prayers... when, just at that moment, the sun appeared brilliant in the eastern sky, centering on me. Fixing my mind on the rising sun, my feelings deepened and my prayers became more concentrated in their devotion. Then suddenly in a moment I felt that my heart was pierced by a ray of white brilliance that filled the whole of Heaven and Earth. I felt my full self wrapped in the great *yōki* of joyousness of the sun. Elated by feelings of gratitude, my mouth flew open in amazement and I swallowed down the rays of the sun.

What happened next was wondrous! The great orb of the sun soared down into my body and heart. The sun and I, I and the sun, became absolutely one. And there in the ecstasy of selflessness I realized the wonderful truth that Kami and man are never two. I had become fully enlightened, knowing the Great Way of eternal immortality, the abiding life that all may share with all of Heaven and Earth.

Kurozumikyō followers revere this sacred event as the "Direct Bestowal of Divine Mission." It was in this experience that Munetada fully comprehended in himself the Way of Amaterasu Ōmikami and was given the mandate to proclaim that Way to others.

Let us look at how some of those to whom Munetada directly taught the Way referred to this experience. Hoshijima's *Short Biography* relates:

It was on the day of the winter solstice of that year when our Founder, while offering his usual prayers to the deity of the sun, was pierced in the breast by *yōki*, the radiant light of the sun. His mouth, spontaneously open with feelings of gratitude and joy, drank in the sun's radiance. His heart all at once was filled with cheerfulness and liveliness, and he realized for himself for the first time how all of heaven and earth works together as a vibrant living being. This happened when the Founder was 35 years of age.

Hoshijima also comments:

On the 11th day of the 11th month, the day of the winter solstice, our Founder, while performing *nippai*, was enlightened to know the Kami of the sun as an active living being. It was at this time that Amaterasu Ōmikami bestowed the Divine Mission upon him. By following the path of filial piety, the Way was opened on the occasion of this Third Auspicious *Nippai*, building upon the first and the second since his illness. In selflessness he became one with the Sun Kami.

The high disciple Kawakami Chūsho tells the story as follows:

> While he was praying to Amaterasu Ōmikami, something from the sun shone upon him, striking and penetrating his chest. He didn't realize it was something from the sun, he only knew that something pierced him right in the chest. Just then he became aware of feeling invigorated, a delightful sensation that was beyond compare. To speak of layers of clouds and fog suddenly clearing from the sky, giving a view of Heaven and Earth in their beautiful serenity, would be to use words for an experience that went far beyond any such description.

Jikihara Ihachiro related the Founder's experience this way:

> Worshiping the great Kami of the sun, not taking his eyes from that solar mirror, he prayed with whole-hearted devotion. Forgetting even his body, selfless and serene, his heart entered the sun itself, where he was lost in total rapture for some time. He had no idea what was happening. The sun-rays of Amaterasu Ōmikami, resembling lightning, resembling a rope, penetrating his chest and stopping in his soul, were becoming, he felt, one with his own heart.
>
> In this way his heart was transformed and he felt very peaceful. Spontaneously, his heart was filled with the joy of life. He knew that Heaven and Earth remained unchanged from the past until now, and that he also remained unchanged in time. He knew then that he had been born of the Kami of the sun, and that from the beginning we have been of one body and of one soul with Kami, with no separation existing between them. This was true not only for himself, but for everything else in Heaven and Earth. Death does not exist. He would exist for all eternity. After birth there would be eternal life. He could remember hearing these things explained at length in what seemed to be the actual voice of Kami.

The Direct Bestowal of his Divine Mission was an event that took place in an instant, it is something which was virtually impossible to communicate fully in either spoken or written words. This last quotation is from a collection of things the Founder told his followers which were repeated by them in their teaching and written down later on, and some minor points may vary slightly depending on the disciple, but there are no discrepancies in basic meaning. The experience did happen when he was 35 years old.

Principles of the Faith

The faith of the Founder centers entirely on Amaterasu Ōmikami. It is Amaterasu, the "round spirit" and mother of the universe, symbolized by the sun, who created everything in the world and is the vital force of the entire universe. She is the great parent of Heaven and Earth. As is written in *Gobun* 249[37] of Munetada's teachings:

Amaterasu Ōmikami created all that exists. Because of Kami, all within heaven and earth lives, so that there is nothing that is impossible to those whose inner self *(kokoro)* is one with her inner self.

Again, there is an *uta* (poem, or song) in *Gobun* 85 that says:

Amaterasu
    With her divine goodness
        And that alone
Plenished heaven and earth
    With these endless blessings.

In this way Munetada sings of Heaven and Earth.

In the Founder Munetada's view, the deity from whom he received his Divine Mission was the greatest in all the universe. In addition, we must remember that Munetada was raised in a family who for generations had served as priests to the Imamura Shrine where Amaterasu Ōmikami was enshrined. This must also have served to reinforce his idea of Amaterasu Ōmikami as the greatest deity in all the universe; from an early age he had held that name in reverence.

This teaching about Amaterasu was distinctly different from Japanese folk beliefs in the Founder's time. There is some basis for this difference in the ancient books of Japan, where the kami Ame-no-Minaka-Nushi-no-Kami is believed to have created everything in the universe. Munetada, however, taught that in the beginning we humans were especially given our own individual souls by Amaterasu Ōmikami, thereby making us one body and one soul with the Kami *(Gobun* 249). This was a universal deity, one for all people, and the resultant faith was also, naturally, for all people.

We may put it this way: Kurozumikyō, though based on the existing beliefs of Japanese people, was developed and elevated by Munetada into a universal creed for all people.

Amaterasu Ōmikami, the mother of the universe, is the vibrant source of life who gave birth to all things. This means that the entire world is therefore filled with the vital energy *(yōki*) of the Way of Amaterasu Ōmikami. Everything is guided by this vital force in accordance with the will of the Sun Kami and thus is joined in universal prosperity. Though it may seem as though there are numerous hardships in life, when properly understood these all happen within the will of Amaterasu. If we accept this and live our lives accordingly, we will undoubtedly come to see our troubles not as troubles at all, but as true prosperity and genuine happiness.

We humans received our hearts and bodies from Amaterasu Ōmikami *(Gobun* 26). Because she is the source of our individual hearts, if we keep that heart in the same state as when we received it, then not the slightest distance will exist between ourselves and Kami. However, due to many

clouds[38] we become separated and the vision of that original state of
existence is lost. Those clouds are our own attachments, our greed,
worries, depression, and indignation. By clearing them away, our hearts
may each return to their original form. Provided that we sustain this state,
we will, indeed, exist as one with Amaterasu Ōmikami. This state of
existence, maintained in oneness in this body without separation, is called
immortality or "abiding life," *(ikidōshi)*, the "original condition" in which
we were created.

The great heart of Amaterasu Ōmikami desires for us a life of prosperity
and wishes to save us from hardships and illness. This great heart is known
as "Sacred Desire" *(Goshinryo)*.[39] Regrettably, our selfish human ego
brings us to misfortune and disaster. However, Munetada received
unequalled divine virtue and strength through the Direct Bestowal of his
Divine Mission. This was due both to his character and devout religious
practices and to the Sacred Desire of Amaterasu Ōmikami. Thus, he was
given the task of proclaiming the Way for the salvation of all people.

This point was powerfully made by the poetic inscription placed by the
high disciple Kawakami on a portrait of the Founder. It reads:

> Disclose the Round Spirit,
> Grasp the handle of all creation.[40]

From childhood on the Founder had wholeheartedly followed the path
of a dutiful son, and, growing up, made his life's goal becoming a living
kami. What Amaterasu Ōmikami communicated in bestowing the Divine
Mission on Munetada was that though people had all originally been given
a virtuous heart, they had subsequently gone in a selfish *(ga)* and harmful
direction. This grieved the Sun Kami, and because she could not bear her
grief at hearing the cries of suffering people she entrusted Munetada with
the mandate to relieve their pains and worries.

Among the poems of the Founder are:

> That vast treasure
>   Which continues to grow
>   Through Heaven and Earth
> Now flows into my own heart
>   Filling it with much joy.

and

> It is my wish
>   To have Amaterasu's
>   Blessings be known
> To all the world's people
>   Soon and without exception.

Chapter Four

Proclaiming the Way

Deciding to Proclaim the Way

With the Direct Bestowal of His Divine Mission as the turning point, the world completely changed for Kurozumi Munetada. He had an entirely new way of thinking that affected everything he did. According to Kawakami's *Biography*, this is how the Founder recalled his experience:

> After receiving the Divine Mission I found joy and pleasure in everything I saw and heard. This was because everything was as clear to me as if I saw it in direct sunlight. I could distinguish everything as clearly as if I were separating the black stones from the white ones used in the game of Go,[41] without hesitation, confusion, or mistake. I could see the reasons behind all that I saw or experienced; nothing was unclear or vague to me.
>
> I realized that if I were to tell anyone about my state of mind, they would surely have taken me as a fool or thought I had lost my mind. I thought it might be wise to hide what had happened and keep it a secret from others for a while.
>
> On second thought, however, I realized that I must comply with the blessing of Amaterasu Ōmikami, and cultivate myself accordingly so as to help others. Both the blessing and the responsibility of my mandate are so awesome that it would be against the divine will if I were to enjoy the blessing only by myself or for myself. It would be against the divine intention *(Goshinryo)* and would trouble the mind of the Great Kami. So, I must from then on have as my set goal in life to liberate countless people from their sufferings by means of the Way the Great Kami had shown me. The objective is to provide comfort, joy, and happiness to their lives.

This account is cited from a written source, but even in the oral tradition concerning the Founder, some believed at the time that the "filial child of

Nakano" had, after recovering from a long and painful illness, lost his mind. For several days neighborhood people expressed their sympathy to his wife as Munetada's loud laughing could be heard by passersby. Such stories were just part of what was said at the time and we cannot know for certain if they are authentic. What is doubtless, however, is that the Founder was overwhelmed with the joy of his enlightenment.

The source of this great joy, of course, was the mission of Amaterasu Omikami that he had received. Through the Way he had been granted he would go forth bringing salvation not just to himself but also to others. This all happened towards the end of the year 1814.

During the days when Munetada was feeling this great joy, and while he was pondering the mission that had been entrusted to him, the following incident happened.

One day, Munetada returned home to find that the young girl serving the Kurozumi family, whose name was Miki, had suddenly come down with severe abdominal pains. Seeing her suffer so, the Founder said, "Ah, such a pity..." In sympathy and without particular forethought he approached her side and put his hands over her lower abdomen. At the same time he blew onto the painful area a strong breath of air which was actually the same *yōki*, or vital energy, that had been entrusted to him by Amaterasu Omikami.[42] Instantly Miki's pain subsided.

The Founder then realized immediately that what had saved him could also be used to benefit others. It was the first time this had happened, and it established him in the confidence he needed that he was not mistaken in his faith and belief. This healing of Miki became known as the first example of *kinen*, or *majinai*;[43] it was the first of many such healings to follow.

At this time, he firmly instructed Miki not to say anything about it to others, nor did he speak of it to others himself. He told her that the healing was not due to any gift of his own but that gratitude was due to Amaterasu Omikami from whose divine virtue the power came. He actually felt there was nothing strange or miraculous about the occurrence and instructed her to keep quiet about it. His way of handling it showed a real humility.

The next morning, however, some neighbors, seeing Miki going about her work as usual after having been so ill, thought it a little strange and began to question her about her recovery. Now Miki, even though she had agreed to say nothing, still thought the event rather incredible. No doubt she also felt that the master of the house was a most remarkable person, and, perhaps out of pride, eventually told the whole story about her healing.

The neighbors were amazed at Miki's complete recovery, but even if she had said nothing they would have begun to watch the Kurozumi house with increased admiration. Munetada's own amazing recovery from hopeless illness and the other unusual things that had been happening opened their eyes to something extraordinary. Word was starting to spread far and wide.

Now near to the northwest of Nakano there was a small hamlet known as Taketōshi where an eye disease was running rampant. The victims of the eye disease, hearing about Miki's recovery, came to the Kurozumi house requesting *majinai* treatment. At first the Founder declined. He didn't even want the event concerning Miki to be talked about. There was, however, a certain man by the name of Ono Eizaburō, an old friend of his and the village headman, who earnestly pleaded on behalf of these sick people. After a while the Founder consented and the *majinai* was performed. He did it in exactly the same way as he had done with Miki: he put his hands on the affected part and blew with a vigorous spirit *(daiyōki)*. This ritual is an act which sprang from his own heart and he did not forget how that inspiration originated. The rite of *majinai* has from that time forward always been carried out in this set form.

Needless to say, the patients recovered and the significance of the healing ritual was confirmed.

After the Founder's Direct Bestowal of Divine Mission he had considerable confidence in the importance of his experience. This confidence increased after his experience of performing *majinai* on Miki, but he still did not allow himself to become publicly active in exercising his power. It wasn't until he performed *majinai* on the villagers of Taketōshi that he gained complete confidence in this method of healing and avowed it as an expression of the divine mission entrusted to him. News of the healing of those with eye disease came to be widely known, and sick people, people in pain, gathered from all over requesting the same help.

It was at this point that Munetada fully decided to propagate the Way. It is important to note that when The Divine Founder began to perform *majinai* to people who sought it he also taught them. He did so in a kindly manner, showing them how they could cultivate and maintain their inner hearts. Proclaiming the Way was from the beginning a movement for spiritual as well as physical renewal.

Sermons and Healing

When those suffering from diseases and troubles, and those seeking the Way, started to come one after another to the Founder's home, it became impossible to speak to them all individually while giving individual *majinai*. So, he would invite them to meet as a group so he could address them together. The subject of these talks was reverence for the Divine Will of Amaterasu Omikami, gratitude for divine blessings, how to avoid injury to the inner spirit and to nurture happy and optimistic feelings, and so on. At the end of each sermon he would heal people by use of *majinai*. These talks came to be known as our Founder's sermons *(kōshaku)*. It was at this time, also, that the first formal disciple, Ono Eizabur, made his pledge.

These talks are really the beginning of the regularly scheduled meeting days *(kaijitsu)* that are held today. It is believed they were started sometime in the spring of 1815. Quite soon after the earliest beginnings, such meetings were held regularly six times a month on days that ended in a "2" or a "7": the second, 12th, and 22nd, and the seventh, 17th, and 27th, of each month.

The Founder's talks were lively and spontaneous. More than this, they are considered to be divinely inspired *(Tengen)*. They did not follow any rules of deliverance and were free,[44] even free from his own opinion. What he said was in words which sprang directly from Amaterasu Ōmikami, untouched by any self-seeking on his part. The words flowed directly from the inner microcosm of deity *(bunshin)*[45] within him, so that what he said was divine and alive.

Several times it happened that he mounted the speaker's seat to deliver a sermon, drank some sacred water, and merely said, "Everyone, thank you very much..." Saying nothing more, he then came down again. On one such occasion the person who had invited him to speak was a bit concerned and asked him to say a little more. But the Founder replied, "As to sermons, there is nothing that I, this Sakyo, can do."

Healing Illness and Pain

A poem in Chinese by one of the Founder's High Disciples, Kawakami Chūsho, deals with how he healed body and spirit at the same time:

> Relieved instantly are pains and
>   troubles in the body.
> Lightened the darkness
>   of selfishness in an instant.
> Changed and nourished the hearts of
>   the idle and wicked for better.
> Once touched by warm divine virtue,
>   Invalids coming in on carts,
> Left for home cured and on foot.[46]

We can see that a sick person is not merely sick in body but also sick in heart. When the Founder treated a person he or she not only became well physically but also changed in character. According to a letter he wrote to Ishio, an important disciple, in 1828:

> In Tatsumi [a nearby hamlet] lives a wealthy farmer by the name of Kameyama Heiroku. Recently he became a believer. He has a younger sister aged seventeen who on the eighth day of this month came down with

convulsions after suffering from chicken pox. Her doctor is Dr. Kishida Kampei of Seno. He is quite well known. He treated her in many ways, but the convulsions only increased.

She had reached the point where she was breathing with difficulty and was barely alive when I called on her and lay my hands upon her. She felt immediate relief and later was able to stop taking all medication. I continued to give her *majinai* two or three times and she is now completely cured. Her condition was so surprisingly better that the commotion in the neighborhood about her illness ceased like the dying of the wind. Such an unusual event causes me to feel so much gratitude to Amaterasu. It is not due to any power of my own. It can only be attributed to a blessing of Nature.

Gobun 72

Again, in the 11th month of 1830 the Founder wrote about his experience with a certain elderly gentleman named Fukuda:

Mr. Fukuda suffered from a serious and prolonged illness and on three occasions appeared to have actually died. Yet, when I prayed deeply to the kami of Heaven and the kami of Earth on his behalf, he experienced a miraculous recovery. In deep gratitude and joy I wrote the following poem:

Never anyone
returning from death three times
to live again...
Not in China, India,
nor in our own Japan.[47]

However, towards the end of autumn of this year, he was stricken as he had been the year before, and his condition worsened by the day. It was difficult to see him suffer so, so on one occasion I told him if he were to let his heart become one with Amaterasu Ōmikami he would experience abiding life *(ikidōshi)*.[48] He accepted this with gratitude, and, as he did, his illness was forgotten and his health began improving day by day. In deep gratitude I sang:

Whenever the heart
of Amaterasu
and a person's heart
Are joined together as one —
This is the Abiding Life.
Miscellany 3

About this there is also the Founder's letter in 1828 to a disciple named Ichimori:

Ito Sahyoe, a Bizen clan samurai, became seriously ill around the fifth month of this year. He had been suffering from pyrosis for 26 years, and had

tried a number of things over those years to alleviate his condition. About
the fourth or fifth month his condition worsened and treatment did not help.
He was unable to eat anything and death seemed certain.

When he had come to the point of accepting death, I went to see him at
the request of his relatives and friends to perform *majinai* on him. I saw that
it was quite understandable that he was accepting death since he could no
longer eat food or take medicine. However, I taught him according to the
Great Way, namely that since the bodily form is subject to illness we should
accept it just as it is and not be troubled in mind or worried about it.

Instead, he should allow his heart to be at one with Amaterasu Ōmikami.
If he did that, he would be purified within and his heart would be cured.
Once the heart is healed, the body will follow.

On hearing this explanation from me, Itoh was blessed with divine grace
and quickly recovered from the illness which had lasted 26 years.

Gobun 74

There is also the case of a man named Ogata Chōjiro of Kamiyamada,
east of Okayama. He had come down with tuberculosis while still young.
At the point that it seemed recovery was impossible, some neighbors
persuaded him to go over to Omoto to see the Founder and worship there.
Ogata felt very hopeful as they all went together to a meeting *(kaijitsu),* and
he attended meetings there without fail for a whole year. However, he was
unable to find a personal blessing of healing to be grateful for. Finally
Ogata decided to ask to be excused from attending any more, and went to
the Founder to bid farewell.

Ogata said, "I do thank you for your patience in permitting me to be here over
this long period of time. I have not received anything like a blessing, and
for the time being at least I would like to be excused. I have seen with my
own eyes person after person receiving the blessing of healing, and I do
believe in such blessings, but I have not been able to receive one myself..."

Upon hearing this the Founder merely said, "Now Ogata san, are you
saying you are giving in to your illness?"

That was all he needed to say. Ogata, feeling as though he had been struck
by lightning, became aware of a strange feeling of being internally purified.
From that day he showed quick improvement and in time he was completely
healed. Later, accompanying the High Disciple Tokio, he helped carry the
message to Harima [near Himeji in present-day Hyōgo Prefecture] where
they were responsible for the salvation of many people.

Tales of the Founder 39

It is next to impossible for us humans to live our lives without ever
becoming sick. Even at the present time, with all the advances we have in
medicine, hospitals everywhere are filled to capacity. In the age of the
Founder, the people who were easiest to reach with the good news of the

Way were those who were ill. Stories about the sick receiving blessings are related in all the books of our teachings. Such stories are especially numerous in the work entitled *Tales of the Founder*.

The Way of Amaterasu Ōmikami is the way of vibrant life *(ikidōshi)* . It is not strange at all that the sick are healed, rather, "it is a natural result of their faith" *(Gobun* 11). The Founder performed *majinai* on the sick one after another and prayed for them, but it was never intended that the purpose of all this was merely healing physical illness. He frequently said, "Illness is the entrance to the Way...," and "My Way is not a way of healing the bodily form, it is a way of healing the heart." The *Short Biography* contains this quotation:

> To those who wanted to receive *majinai*, I blew upon them the breath of *yōki* and then spoke to them about how to care for their hearts. Serious illnesses and prolonged sicknesses are quickly cured. With the healing of their sicknesses people can be led into the Way's greatness.

So, we can see that actually the healing of an illness and the healing of the heart are one and the same thing. The real purpose is to be bathed in the divine blessings of Amaterasu Ōmikami so that one can live a life of gratitude and joy. In this way it is made possible for us to live in the Way of Amaterasu. This, then, is the message that should be remembered.

Meeting Days

The meeting days at the time of the Founder have been described by a direct disciple, a farmer named Imada Esaji, in a written account. It is believed that he was referring to a period that falls sometime between 1844 and 1848. He writes:

> The meetings on the "two and seven" days were well attended. We rarely failed to go, but there were others who came from even greater distances and who had to return home again that same night. In those days there was a sword rack at the entrance and a number of swords were placed there. It looked very impressive, but we took off our straw raincoats and put them down next to the rack anyway before entering the house. The place was filled with worshipers, including some from leading samurai families in service to the Ikeda clan, such as the Furutas and the Ishidas.
>
> There was no segregation, however, in which one person was given an upper seat of honor because he was a samurai, or another had to sit in a less desirable seat because he was a farmer. No matter who it was, even a merchant or an artisan, it was the first person who arrived that got the best seat. All were seated in the order that they arrived.

On this particular day it seemed that some important people had to sit in inconvenient places on the floor, with low-born people bowing to them as they arrived, while low-born women and children sat up in the better seats. The samurai had much authority at that time and were generally keen on their dignity, but at these meetings they often could neither get outside if they needed to nor see very well.

Once the meeting began there was absolute silence. Once in a while you could hear the clap of hands *(kashiwade)*[49] but that was all. No noise came from anyone, even the women and children. But this was not caused by any kind of rigid formality. The voice of the Founder sank into us, deep into our hearts. We were so deeply moved that our heads became heavy and we felt nothing but gratitude and the sanctity of the moment.

Once the meeting was over, we could not remember anything that had been said, and I have an excellent memory about everything else. Until I was about sixty or so I could even remember the time at which small things happened long ago. I was called a "living diary." But I could not remember anything said by the Founder at one of those meetings. Of course, I came to understand that it was not necessary to remember what was said. That was not the point. It was important simply to be filled with gratitude.

After the sermon there was *majinai* for those who had asked for it, again on a first-come-first-served basis. Those who needed healing were lying down, ready to be helped. After that we all partook of a dinner together, and then the meeting was considered to be over. This was usually around ten at night.

Afterwards everyone mingled together freely. The Founder treated everyone equally in a free and friendly fashion, with the sick getting special and careful attention. As a result, whenever the followers happened to meet somewhere it was like meeting members of a family. We enjoyed a feeling of mutual closeness and care for each other.

On one occasion as I was returning home from a meeting I happened to meet five or six samurai. They were ahead of me on the path and also going home from the same meeting. I was going along behind them for a while when they turned and asked me very politely how far I had to go. When I answered that I was going to Shimoyamada in Oku county they apologized for holding me up when I had so far to go and urged me to go on ahead of them, relinquishing their rightful place on the road to me, a farmer. This was, I knew, because of the Way, and I felt deeply grateful.

Now Shimoyamada is more than 20 kilometers from Omoto where the meetings were held, and some people like Mr. Imada attended by walking that distance and returning in a single day. We must realize also how epoch-making it was in this period of history, in which there was such a rigid division of classes of society into samurai, farmers, artisans, and merchants, that they actually used the system of first-come-first-served seating.

This account also makes it possible for us to visualize the pattern of real camaraderie and friendship that existed among the followers. The people who came to listen to the Founder were most serious and devoted, and the atmosphere of the meetings was quite calm and peaceful.

As seen through the eyes of the Founder, there was no distinction at all between those of various occupations, or between men and women, the young and the old. All were equally children of Amaterasu Ōmikami, and he befriended and taught them all equally.

Missionary Activity beyond Omoto

It appears that in the spring of 1815 there was an increase not only in the number of followers but also in the number of other people coming to worship or to pay respects. In addition to the regular meeting days established at the Founder's home, he would on other days also go out to other places in response to their requests to visit and to speak. Eventually lecture halls *(kōseki)* were established here and there to serve this growing need. We know from early records and memos that the Founder established a schedule by which he went out daily, sometimes near and sometimes quite far. On some days he would go out to teach and to heal two or even three times.

The order of events in these newly established places was the same as in his home: he would give sermons and then perform *majinai.* However, the composition of those who attended varied somewhat from that in his home. As had been pointed out, those who attended there were people from all classes of society. The lecture halls in other places, however, each seem to have taken on some special characteristics of their own.

For example, in Banchō, which was one of the residential quarters of Ikeda clan samurai, there was a meeting in which several samurai took turns serving as host, always in one of their homes. They called themselves the "rice-cleaning meeting" *(kome-tsuki)* to show that their activity in meeting together improved the process of going from an unpolished to a polished state.[50] A great many samurai attended these meetings although some craftsmen and merchants also used to come.

Meetings in other lecture halls were attended mostly by townsmen *(chōnin),* regarded in those days as the lowest class. Among these, one was called "Nanashima's meeting" after the man who organized it in his store, known simply as the Nanashimaya. Another man, one Rokuzaemon, a maker of roof tiles, hosted a meeting at his factory. The story is that this meeting was held on the first day of each month, and that on the day of the meeting Rokuzaemon himself would go around the neighborhood encouraging people to attend.

Meetings were held also at Shinto shrines and Buddhist temples, as well as at the homes of some village headmen. These places were chosen in order to accommodate the large number of people who attended and received blessings together.

Whatever the place in which a meeting was held, the spreading of the teachings in lecture halls happened because individuals took responsibility to set them up, either in their own homes or in space they found elsewhere. Motivations to do this were many. In some cases there was someone who wanted blessings from the Founder, in order to have a family member be healed or to bring better fortune to an unhappy or an unfortunate home. In other cases a lecture hall was provided by someone who had already received a blessing from the Founder and wanted to show appreciation by bringing knowledge of the Way to others in their neighborhood. Through these meetings the Great Way spread steadily.

Obstacles in Propagating the Religion

Occasionally there were people who objected to the Founder's activity and placed obstacles in his way. We can see the deeper character of his teaching from the way he met these difficulties. A memorandum he wrote to the ranking priest of the Imamura Shrine, known as Imamura Nakaba, gives us considerable insight into these matters. It was a statement submitted in the third month of 1816, about a year after the first disciple was accepted. It was entitled "A Written Memorandum Concerning Missionary Work," and reads as follows:

1. It is true that I have been performing *majinai*, both here at home for people who came asking for it and at other places when I am invited there to hold meetings. On these occasions I speak in ordinary language about matters of everyday living and about the attitude we should have in living our lives, and then I perform *majinai*.

    I am very careful in the words I use. Never do I make reference to subjects that could hurt other people's feelings or cause difficulties. Neither do I say things that could be taken as boasting. I do not allow others, even those close to me, to spread rumors in praise of me or to give me a high reputation.

2. From now on, no matter what the social status may be of those who invite me to speak and ask me for treatment, I will not permit myself to be praised by them or by others who attend. I will be guided by these rules in everyday activity.

3. Although in the past I have presented *omamori*[51] to those who requested *majinai* treatment, I will not do this in the future at my own discretion. There are regulations about who may distribute *omamori* and when I thoughtlessly disobeyed them it was conduct contrary to clan regulations. I am indeed very sorry that I disregarded your authority.

    Although I should have stopped distributing them immediately, I am most grateful that by special arrangement with your office and the clan authorities, the matter can now be left behind us and the distribution regarded as though done through the priestly family.

I faithfully promise that from now on I will strictly and honestly follow all clan rules and your instructions in every detail. There will be not the slightest doubt of our obedience to the rules. In witness to all this the undersigned has written this as an expression of our full understanding. No other understanding exists apart from what has been written.

This document is extremely important for us in a number of ways. In terms of the content of the teachings, we can see in the statement the emphasis on watchwords for everyday living. The guideposts for faith were guideposts for life. In order to live a happy life, a life filled with contentment and free from afflictions and suffering, we must live it in accordance with the heart of Amaterasu Ōmikami. Deepening faith in that heart has its effect in how we live our daily lives. This teaching was the constant theme of the Founder, and is today still the spiritual foundation of Kurozumikyō.

We can also see something about how the teachings were spreading. The memorandum shows there were objections about the use of *omamori,* but we can see this was just an excuse. The real reason for the objections was the high popularity of the Founder and the numbers of the followers he had gained in less than a year from the time he started teaching. Believers had increased in great numbers, and it was for this reason he was bitterly attacked by the chief priest of the shrine.

Still, the disagreement seems to have had an effect on his activities. Five years later, in 1821, he wrote to the Okayama samurai, Ishio Kensuke, who was on duty in Edo (Tokyo), saying:

> This Way I teach has shown quite a change from when you left. I feel it had expanded a little too quickly and too far. Now we are being more moderate and controlling our efforts better in propagating the Way.
>
> *Gobun* 3

From this letter we can gather that a lot more people were hearing his teachings and becoming members. However, this brought with it a certain amount of slander and abuse from outsiders. The Founder wrote again to Ishio in 1823:

> The Way appears to be flourishing more and more. But because it has expanded beyond our expectation, there are doctors and faith healers who are circulating groundless rumors and pure fabrications about us. We hear this repeatedly, including from the authorities. It reminds us of the saying "evil deeds quickly go a thousand miles."
>
> There are doctors and faith healers and others who align themselves with them, and priests of the Nichiren sect, who are unhappy to hear about the

many sick who are receiving blessings and the many who are worshiping with us. They are taking advantage of the situation and are criticizing and condemning our faith.

Since these are groundless stories, the authorities don't seem to attach any importance to them. But there are some who don't know what is really going on or who don't have good judgement and are hesitant to come to our meetings *(kaijitsu)* in Omoto. Despite all this the number of worshipers is increasing; there are more than ever before. I am grateful that I am able to use these adversities as raw material for my spiritual training, deepening my faith and serving to promote the Great Way.

Gobun 28

The attitude of the Founder toward this slander and persecution was never to blame others for the wrong they had done. Instead, he used those things as occasions to reflect on his own conduct. He regarded them as a means for his own religious practice.

It was probably around this time that the following event happened. One morning the Founder went out into his garden and saw that his roof was scorched in several places. It was quite obvious that these burnt places were caused by someone trying to set fire to his home. Later, looking around, he found the torch that the guilty person had used in the arson attempt. He then cleaned and purified it and put it in his home shrine as an offering to Amaterasu Omikami.

"What a frightening thing to have happened!" he said. It was the law at the time that an arson offender, if he were caught, would be burned at the stake. But, even more serious in the Founder's view was the damage the arsonist would do to his own inner soul *(bunshin)*, his connection with Amaterasu. For the Founder such punishment would be unthinkable.

Fortunately no serious damage was done to the house, and he felt that this was a blessing not only to himself but also to the person and his family. "I am so grateful," he said in praise to Amaterasu. And with such thanks the Founder then prayed that the man would have a change of heart and return to being a good person once again.

He prayed with wholehearted devotion for a period of three weeks in behalf of the man who tried to burn down his house. What he prayed for was that the man would have a change of heart and that he would be become able to improve himself. Then, three weeks from the day he began his prayers, the man in question did appear at the Founder's home. Unable to endure his pangs of conscience, he confessed all and begged forgiveness.

The Founder spoke to him about the Way and after encouraging him to exert himself for the sake of the Way, forgave him of his deed. In a kind manner the Founder revived the man's heart and provided inspiration to his life. It is also said that the man, with tears of repentance, eventually signed a pledge and became a grateful follower of the Way. What was meant as an objection to the Founder's work was turned into an occasion for the spreading of the Way.

The Direct Disciples I

The disciples who received teachings under the Founder during his lifetime are known as "Direct Disciples" *(Gojikimon)*. The first person who became a disciple *(monjin)*[52] was Ono Eizaburō, who during the first month of 1815 declared himself to be a follower of the Way by presenting to the Founder a written "divine pledge" *(shinmon)*. In return for this lifelong vow he was accepted as a disciple. The pledge states:

Divine Pledge

To: Kurozumi *Sensei*[53]

Herewith I vow most solemnly as I receive initiation from Kurozumi *Sensei* into the Sacred Way that I will henceforth endeavor to abide by its teachings more and more with all my heart. Should I ever by any action turn aside from these teachings I will welcome divine punishment from the Sun, Moon, and Stars. With this intention I hereby submit this written vow.

First month, 1815
Ono Eizaburō

Ono Eizaburō was the first person to offer up such a pledge, but eventually the *Register of Disciples* contained the names of well over a thousand who did so.

It appears that these pledges were given only by the most advanced of the followers. The oral tradition tells us that those special ones among the general membership of believers[54] who had offered up the pledge were known as the "Vowed Society" *(Shinmon Shū)*. The Founder gave these people direct and private instruction.

By their more intensive religious practice they attained mastery of the spiritual condition known as "heaven-heart" *(Ten-shin)*. They were even referred to as *Tenshin* by the Founder. They received general respect as members of the *Tenshin Shū* (Heaven-Heart Society), a title considered to be the highest honor that a disciple could receive.

The content of the individual pledges presented by the many who joined was not uniform. The vow differed somewhat, depending on the individual. Take Aochi Tohshiro for example. He was an Okayama samurai with an income of 300 *koku*[55] of rice. His pledge reads:

Divine Pledge

To Kurozumi *Sensei:*

I hereby gratefully promise to devote myself to religious practice and discipline without bringing disharmony to the true and original heart of all Heaven and Earth.

Aochi Tshiro
(signed)
11th month, 1821

Another example is the pledge of Gōji Shichiemon, an Okayama samurai with an income of 200 *koku,* which reads:

Divine Pledge

To Kurozumi *Sensei:*

In gratitude for our good fortune and having been initiated into the Way of Heaven and Earth and of all Nature, we hereby promise to persist with all our hearts in following these teachings. With this intention we submit this Written Vow.

The second month of 1834
Gōji Shichiemon Katsuoki
Gōji Kura (wife)
Gōji Kimi (daughter)
Gōji Mozaemon Katsuyoshi

While eventually the number of those referred to as the vowed society was something over a thousand, the total number of general believers who received teaching directly from him extended into the tens of thousands, perhaps between 100,000 and 200,000.

Some Prominent Disciples

A few of this large number, especially among those who entered the faith during the *Bunsei* period (1818-1829), are especially worthy of our notice.

Furuta Masanaga (also known as Yujiro; 1791-1850) became a disciple in 1819. He was a samurai of Okayama with an income of 550 *koku* of rice. A samurai of such high rank must have had some remarkable reason for joining the faith, but opinions differ as to what it may have been. It is recorded in the writings of the Founder, however (*Gobun* 21), that Furuta attended the meetings without fail. He appears to have been a warm person with deep devotion. That a person of such esteem became a member helped the movement become much more influential in the society of the times.

Another important disciple was the Okayama samurai Ishio Kensuke (1775-1859), with an income of 140 *koku.* He became a disciple in 1821, and is considered the most important of the Four High Disciples. Ishio was five years older than the Founder and their friendship extended over a great many years. With Munetada being the son of the village Shinto priest and Ishio being a parishioner, they knew each other well. They also had a mutual interest in chanting Noh plays,[56] so we can be certain their relationship was quite deep. Most likely Ishio had known the Founder from quite early years.

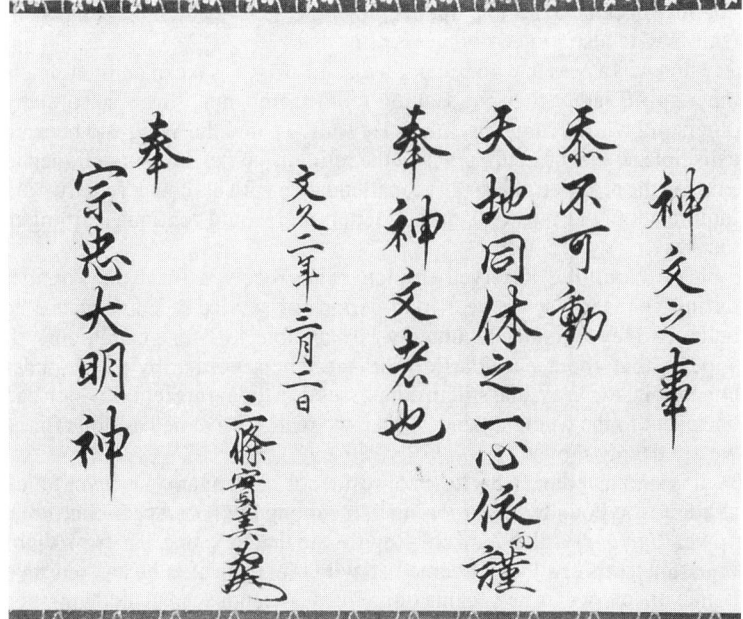

Fig. 5   An example of a vow *(shinmon)* by a follower. This one was made by Prince Sanjyo Sanetomi a few days after the Munetada Shrine in Kyoto was dedicated in 1862. The prince was a member of the imperial household party active in preparing the way for the Meiji Restoration (1867). *Courtesy of Kurozumikyō*

Ishio enjoyed high standing as a person of character even within the ruling Ikeda clan in which he served. He was respected by the head of the clan and by high ranking retainers. We can assume merely from the fact that he was a devout believer that the Kurozumi teachings were not considered to be heretical, at least not within the clan. A possible investigation by clan officials in connection with the *omamori* distribution question mentioned above would of course have been done by men from that group. However, no prohibition of such distribution ever occurred.

Even though the Founder and Ishio were life-long friends, the latter did not become a disciple until after the Direct Bestowal of Divine Mission experience had taken place. Indeed, it was a full eight years after the Founder's revelation that he presented his pledge and was accepted as a disciple. Before that happened the two men merely continued their friendship as usual. When criticisms of the Founder arose, Ishio was not misled. At first he seemed merely to admire him cautiously, but later he not only became a disciple but his father did so as well, in the same year. Ishio's wife also joined two years after that.

Ishio was a person who became a disciple for the sake of cultivating his inner spirit, rather than for seeking relief from some illness as so many others did who became disciples. He truly wanted the Way, and became a disciple so that he could practice the religion. When he was stationed in Edo, on the required alternate-year attendance with his clan lord, he would inquire about the Way by means of letters and would continue learning in that way.

Ishio carefully preserved the letters he received from the Founder during his nearly seven year-long periods of service in Edo because he believed they would undoubtedly be valuable to later generations. It appears that about one-fourth of all the letters written by the Founder concerning the Way, and still in our possession today, are letters which had been sent to the disciple Ishio. When we realize what he has done for us we are deeply moved.

It is said that during his times of residence in Okayama he never failed to attend the Founder's sermons and, receiving *majinai*, experience great power *(daiyōki)* within himself. Reports are that he spoke of a warm vigor imparted to his heart which remained with him even after he had returned home. In later years he became quite ill, and friends who visited him then were surprised to hear him chanting Noh plays in a rich clear voice. Thinking it most unusual, they would ask him about his illness, to which he would reply, "Illness is illness. Chanting is chanting."

He indeed put into practice, with all the strength of his faith, a major concept of the Founder's teachings: "Don't let the heart be swayed by illness in the physical form. Let the heart rather make use of the physical form."

Being a samurai, Ishio did not engage in extensive preaching himself, but he did occasionally give lectures on the Way in his home. His family, too, were believers. There are also stories about him that have been handed down concerning his ability, when going out on other business, to perform *majinai* and to transmit blessings upon others. He passed away in 1859 at the age of 85.

Hishikawa Ginzaburō (1773-1849), generally known as Ginjibei, became a disciple in 1821.[57] He was a sexton at a Buddhist temple near Kunitomi in Okayama. One day he was out delivering *omamori* from his temple when he happened to come across a lecture hall where the Founder was speaking. As he listened to the lecture he felt as if he had wakened from a dream of many years. He felt strongly that he had found the person that he could entrust with his life. He immediately made preparations to be accepted as a disciple, reaching the Founder's home to do so even before Munetada got home from the meeting.

From that time on he never left the Founder's side, serving him with commitment and devotion. He not only aided the Founder in personal ways, but also helped as an attendant at lectures. In the home he willingly took on some of the less pleasant tasks around the house.

Ginjibei is not included in the list of the Four High Disciples. However, in the depth of his understanding and in his ability to carry out what he knew, he was not one step behind anyone. There are a great number of stories that have been handed down about this old man. Nearly all of them show him to be most lovable and unique in character. Towards the end of his life he expressed a desire to be allowed to die at the feet of his *Sensei,* and in the eighth month of 1849 this was more than fulfilled. He passed away with his head in the Founder's lap.

In 1822 the foremost scholar of Chinese classics in the Bizen area, later considered as one of the Four High Disciples, Kawakami Chūsho, became a member. Kawakami's name does not appear in a record of disciples[58] which lists the names of the Kurozumi members. However, the *Chronology of the Founder's Life* which he prepared shows the names of these four, including his name, along with the dates on which they became members. Kawakami was a scholar of the Wang Yang-ming school of learning and was known throughout Japan for his scholarship. He had studied under Sato Issai (1772-1859) and it is said that he was close friends with other well-known scholars such as Oshio Chusai (1793-1837), a well-placed legal official in Osaka.[59]

Now it happened that Kawakami's mother, the Lady Tsuyako, suffered from an eye ailment, and although she tried a number of different treatments they all failed and she eventually lost her sight. Kawakami, always a most dutiful son towards his mother, wanted desperately to find a cure for her disease. Encouraged by a friend, he attended one of the

Founder's meetings *(kaijitsu)*. Later, in the preface of his book *Texts for a New Mission,* he wrote at length about the time in his life that led up to the eventual blessing of his mother in which she regained her eyesight. He says clearly that it was the healing of his mother that motivated him to become a disciple.

But it was not easy for him, at first anyway, quickly and meekly to accept the words of Munetada. Being a scholar of Wang Yang-ming and of the science of divination, Kawakami had a number of preconceived opinions. It was only after he had gone to hear sermons three times that he was able to abandon his preconceptions and permit himself to move toward being accepted into the Founder's fold.

At the time that his mother regained her eyesight, Kawakami wrote a letter to the Founder expressing his deep gratitude and joy. This letter, known as the "Second New Year's Letter" reflects his thankfulness. It reads in part:

> I am grateful to have been initiated into the teaching of Amaterasu Ōmikami. I would never have been able to enjoy this salvation of mine without the teaching of Kurozumi *Sensei.* I understand the grace of Kami much more because of the favor *(on)* of the *Sensei.* You guided me kindly so I may know for myself the blessings of the Great Kami. As I sit quietly in meditation in my study on this rainy day, my tears flow down my cheeks in my feeling of gratitude. Please accept the deep sincerity of my heart and bestow your generous understanding upon me.

"Second New Year," incidentally, refers to the first day of the "second first month of the year," coming after the added intercalary first month of the fifth year of the *Bunsei*[60] era (1822), in accordance with the lunar calendar then being used. From that time on, for nearly 30 years, Kawakami was in and out of the Founder's home learning deeply from his teachings. He finally died in 1862 at the age of 68.

In 1838 Kawakami wrote another letter which has been preserved. Referred to as "The Letter to Kurozumi *Sensei* Inquiring about the Way of Filial Piety," it says, in outline:

> In almost all matters it is said that "more than enough" is not a good thing. But it is also said that in the matter of filial piety we must strive to do more than enough. Stories from former times dealing with filial piety tell of dutiful children who were nearly always poor and who were praised for striving to be filial by sacrificing themselves in the midst of poverty. This kind of piety was given the highest regard, but I feel that is truly a mistake. There is no parent who is made glad by sacrificing a child. When a child sacrifices himself in order to be filial a parent is not made happy. On the contrary, that parent is made to suffer.

Therefore, I am wondering how it would be to carry out another kind of filial piety, even if some might not call it so, which has as its purpose bringing joy both to parents and to children, both physically and spiritually [rather than going to such lengths of self-sacrifice]. This is an authentic kind of filial piety that I myself would like to follow. However, I will appreciate your candid comments on these points so I will know how to conduct myself.

The Founder's letter which replied to the above concerns has been lost, but Kawakami's serious, thoughtful attitude is clear from this quotation. Questions like these were brought up not by Kawakami alone; many disciples raised similar questions which were presented to the Founder for his advice.

Kawakami was a classical scholar, and left a number of literary works concerning the Way.[61] He wrote them as records of questions asked by people about the Way and his own answers to them. A poem Kawakami left us goes like this:

To those who have not
    viewed the peak of Mt. Fuji
        what can one relate
of how that wonderful form
    mingles with the High Heaven?[62]

In this poem Kawakami is thinking of the divine virtue of the Founder in speaking of Mt. Fuji. To a person who has not seen the mountain it makes no difference at all how much you talk about that splendid form stretching forth in the heavens. There is simply no way for him to comprehend. In the same way there is no way to explain Amaterasu Omikami and her blessing in the form of the Founder, Kurozumi Munetada. It was to such lengths that Kawakami went in revering the virtues of his spiritual teacher.

Kawakami's book *Texts for a New Mission* was written in literary Chinese with the hope that the teachings of the Founder would some day be carried to China. He also wrote a number of Chinese poems, including the one inscribed on a portrait of the Founder painted in 1847 by Matsuda Suigai. This praise poem is regarded as his representative piece of classical writing and is cited in the *Chronology of the Founder's Life*.

These disciples were impressive people, each in a different way. Taken together, they give us a good understanding of the powerful effect produced by Kurozumi Munetada, the Founder, as he proclaimed the Way to others.

Chapter Five

Aspirations and Humility: the Opening Way

In the middle period of Munetada's life he developed his religious capacities even further. His inner purity of spirit — his humility *(kentoku)* — led him to gain ever deeper insight into himself and into others. He gained this insight by learning how to learn from his own daily experience as well as by following a number of more traditional forms of religious practice.[63] Throughout, his aspiration and zeal were guided by his devotion to Amaterasu Ōmikami. As a result, his aspiration and his humility balanced one another in the course of his religious development.

The Good Fortune of Amaterasu Ōmikami

On one of the Founder's pilgrimages to the Ise Shrine he was asked by a Shinto priest what it was he had prayed for. "I simply prayed for the continuing good fortune *(kaiun)*[64] of Amaterasu Ōmikami," he is said to have replied. This indeed was the aspiration to which he devoted himself throughout his life.

Praying for the "good fortune of Amaterasu Ōmikami" meant to him extolling the divine virtues of Kami and hoping that every single person in the world would be awakened to the blessings that would be opened as the Way broadened.

As the individual soul *(bunshin;* the "small spirit," the "divided portion" of Amaterasu within each person) is awakened in each of us we open to the Great Way of Amaterasu (the *honshin;* universal, cosmic Spirit). This was the great purpose of the Founder's prayers at Ise. Having this mission expresses the great fortune he himself had received, entrusted to him by Amaterasu.

His own experience of the opening way is described in his letters:

Lately the wonderful blessings of *majinai* are frequently being manifested, and I am sure this is due to the workings of Heaven and Earth. Such things only happen when I am performing these *majinai*, and I feel gratitude for that. Yet, what has resulted is less than one part of a thousand of what Amaterasu Ōmikami wishes to make possible. Realizing this, I feel most inadequate and sad.

But then I remember that both my heart and my bodily form actually belong to Heaven and Earth, and are part of the natural working of the universe. I am leading my life relying daily on this divine arranging, letting go of all things in accordance with that. This thought brings peace to my heart and to my life, and it is why I strive daily to cultivate my heart.

Gobun 25

Truly I have been granted immense blessings from a boundless Heaven, though I feel so incapable. I am able to fulfill not a hundredth of what has been opened to me. All I can do just now is not to desecrate these biddings by doing anything that is evil or that hurts anyone, or by hurting my own inner spirit. I am grateful there have been a few times lately when I have been able to enter a state of nothingness.[65] At those times I have been able to rise above the dualities of existence and non-existence, and, free from having to insist on the forms of things, to become free of greed and desires. I have come close to the presence of Heaven's power *(ikimono)*.[66] If I continue striving to cultivate my heart I will surely receive the blessings of Heaven.

Gobun 38

In another letter the Founder wrote concerning the good fortune of Amaterasu Ōmikami as follows:

The Way is opening wider and wider and, as it does, my gratitude also grows. We are now receiving invitations from all over asking us to undertake so much service that we cannot respond to more than one in a hundred or a thousand. We are called to all directions to hold meetings *(kōseki)*.

One of the things we are grateful for is that, thanks to Amaterasu, I do not grow weary in this work though I am busy every day. And, miracles do occur almost every day, in various places. We are most grateful that these are auspicious days when the good fortune of Amaterasu Ōmikami is being opened more and more.

When reports come daily telling us of people experiencing the wonder of the divine virtue, I join them in feeling the deepest gratitude to Amaterasu Ōmikami.

Gobun 25

As these letters of the Divine Founder show, "good fortune of Amaterasu Ōmikami" refers to the spreading of the Way each time one more person in the world comes to receive in gratitude the divine blessings.

Humility and Reserve

The Founder's aspiration in proclaiming the Way is clearly stated in the following poem:

> The moon is setting
> and the sun is appearing
> as dawn is breaking,
> Now, indeed, the time has come
> to set out on the Way.[67]
> *O-uta* 133

Here we can see the source of his lively sense of mission. Yet, on the other hand, he had been bestowed with real humility and reserve. This was evident in all of his words and actions in proclaiming the Way. *Gobun* 25 quoted above makes this clear. In another letter he says it even more clearly:

> While I have been initiated into the Way and feel most grateful for that, my lack of strength in carrying it out as completely as Amaterasu wishes is vexing to me.
>
> *Gobun* 39

As the divine blessings increased in number, the Founder's sense of the inadequacy of his religious practice also increased, and he reflected deeply on his ineptness. An incident related in the *Tales of the Founder* explains this point:

> On one occasion a samurai of the Okayama clan by the name of Tokura was blessed by being cured of an illness. His friends were all agreed that it was due to the Founder's virtue and went to him to thank him. But he replied, "This is not because of any virtue of mine. The cause was your own overflowing zeal in wanting to help Tokura, which was conveyed to Kami as true sincerity *(makoto)*.[68] In turn that sincerity was conveyed to me from Heaven and help was then provided."
>
> *Tales of the Founder* 34

Again, in *Gobun* 12 the Founder writes,

> Ishio, here at home your respected father and dear wife, whom you had to leave here in Okayama while you are serving in Edo, are enjoying extremely

good health and on occasion come to Omoto to attend the meeting. They are devoted in the faith and extremely lively and in good spirits. Were you to return now they would seem like different people. But this is in accordance with the workings of Heaven and Earth, and I have done nothing praiseworthy at all myself..."

Gobun 12

The Founder always stressed, as he did here, that the manifestation of divine virtue did not have anything at all to do with his own merits. It was always a case of the sincerity of the people drawing upon the Sincerity of Heaven and Earth.

We have also seen that on those occasions when obstacles were raised by doctors, healers, and Buddhist priests hindering the propagation of the faith, the Founder did not condemn those that slandered him. Even when the truth was clearly on his side he felt that the cause was in his own lack of virtue and he used the occasion as an opportunity for deep self-reflection.

On one occasion some mountain ascetics *(yamabushi)*[69] came to him demanding that he stop his preaching. The Founder, however, did not argue with them. He merely listened to what they had to say (*Tales of the Founder* 26). On the occasion when a certain faith healer tried to set fire to Munetada's house, he merely prayed for this evildoer until the man finally came to his senses (*Tales of the Founder* 1). Concerning a problem he was having with a temple of the Nichiren sect, he wrote:

I don't blame others for their faults and shortcomings. It is better that I myself strive to do what is right. I have no time to dwell on others' actions. Rather, I am constantly concerned that my heart is not more fully in service to Amaterasu's mission, and I have no intention of criticizing anyone else.

Gobun 35

We see from this that the Founder was convinced the best way to spread the Way was first of all to purify his own heart fully. Then he would be able clearly to see how to overcome any kind of obstacles and slanders (*Gobun* 30).

Everyday Life as Religious Discipline

Generally speaking, religious or ascetic practice *(shugyō)* has meant going through various kinds of hardship, such as climbing mountains in winter while dressed in scanty clothing or standing under waterfalls in the dead of winter. To the Founder, however, practice has a different meaning. He put it this way:

When we experience something we enjoy, we should accept it gratefully; and when we find something undesirable or a burden, we should accept it as an opportunity for practice. When we take this approach, there is absolutely nothing that happens that is not an occasion for practice.

Gobun 24

When we carefully consider the basic character of our birth in this world, we realize that since we are all born in a human form we will have difficulties, since that is inherent in having form.

The religious practice I teach is to not regard difficulties as problems but as opportunities to improve ourselves. Then religious practice is not a burden, but rather a time that by the gift of Kami brings us nothing but joy and pleasure. This way of thinking is the essence of the Great Way. As a result, when we live according to the Way, we experience surpassing inner ease *(dai anraku)*.

Thus, we can see that living freely and happily depends simply on our own hearts, on choices we ourselves can make and on how we ourselves look at life.

Gobun 143

We do run into all sorts of problems in our daily lives, but we can accept them as the raw material of our religious practice. In this sense, practice is not something that has a set form that must be adhered to. Rather, it can be understood as coming from within our hearts as we deal with the various things we ordinarily face in life. It is based in an attitude that seeks to remain constant in the face of such problems as sickness, poverty, and conflicts in human relationships; or even in such mundane aspects of daily life as things that happen while eating, bathing, or sleeping.

Once the Founder himself fell seriously ill. This happened in 1823, from the eighth until the 28th days of the sixth month, a period of nearly three weeks. This was after the Direct Bestowal of Divine Mission, of course, and since it was a serious matter of life and death we must pay special attention to what happened. He described his mental attitude at the time as follows:

Sometime ago I was not feeling at all well. I was extremely grateful for your prayers for me, one after another. I myself did not pray for recovery at all at the time. I merely left all things to the care of Heaven. If Kami found me of no more use in this world, then I would be taken away. In the event I could still do something for the sake of the world, I would be cured. Facing my illness with this attitude, I found that I was miraculously healed. I owe this to Amaterasu and am indebted to the Kami's grace.

Den Gobun 2[70]

Only a few years later, Chayamachi Chojirō, his daughter's husband, died of an illness, and his reaction was similar. Even sickness and death are occasions for religious practice given us by Kami. We should be grateful for such hardships as aspects of the Great Way and humbly accept them.

The basis of this acceptance of everything that happens as *shugyō* is an absolute faith in Amaterasu Ōmikami. If we live our lives in a way that is consistent with the heart of Amaterasu Ōmikami, divine parent of us all, nothing that happens will turn out evil or bad. Through our faith we will, without fail, receive divine guidance and assistance. On the surface something may seem inconvenient, painful, uninteresting, or trying, but if we were to see it from the point of view of our parental Kami, we would know that it is not bad at all. With our hearts firm in this faith, we can see that everything will go well for our improvement. The Founder emphasizes to us how we can overcome all illusion and doubt by thinking of all such things as religious practice.

Special Forms of Religious Practice

Not all the practice of the Founder, however, was of this type. He did not ignore in the least those practices which had established form. He performed such observances as daily worship of the rising sun, recitation of the Great Purification Prayer many times, paying visits and offering prayer consecutively at five different Shinto shrines, paying visits and offering prayers at one hundred different shrines within a month, the thousand-day retreat, and the like. He also encouraged others to do these things.

Let us consider these special forms of practice. We will see that each of them became means by which his spirituality was significantly advanced.

Visitation to Five Shrines

In a letter written late in 1823 the Founder wrote that on occasion he would perform the "visit to five shrines." He could do this on a single morning. The five were the Imamuragu where he served, the Shirahigegu situated to the west of that, the Kibitsu Hiko Jinja (also known as the Bizen Ichi no Miya), the Kibitsugu, and the Niwase Daijingu. The distance he covered to do this was just under 20 kilometers. Of course, he made his rounds on foot. Describing this activity he wrote:

> Hearing the seventh bell (4 A.M.) I get up, purify myself with cold water, and get dressed. First of all I pay homage at the Imamuragu. Next I go over to Nakasendō to pray at the Shirahigegu and then continue on to the Bizen Ichi no Miya, and it is still dark. I then continue on to the Kibitsugu and from

there circle around to the Daijingu. It is still not dawn. From there I leave for home and get there before sunrise. I repeat the Great Purification Prayer about 200 times, and then at last the sun starts rising in the east.

The whole thing takes less than an hour. Under normal circumstances it would take a whole day to visit the five shrines, yet it can be done in less than an hour. But, not wanting to cause rumors and the like, I don't really talk about it. Yet this is the pace at which everything I have been doing happens and I am very grateful for the vigor I have been given.

Gobun 31

In this letter the Founder expresses his amazement that he was able to make the rounds of the five shrines in less than an hour. Ordinarily it took a whole day to do all these visits. He adds that he did not always have this experience; it was not something that happened all the time. Yet the speed at which he could do them compares to the pace of a world-class marathon runner. When we consider the fact that he was dressed in the traditional clothing of the Shinto priesthood[71] and also stopped to pray at all the five shrines, our common sense tells us that it was humanly impossible and could be nothing else than miraculous.

There is also a story about the close follower Ginjibei, who decided to accompany the Founder on a morning visit to the five shrines. Finding the Founder's pace much too fast for him, Ginjibei soon raised a cry of distress and politely asked him to slow down. But the Founder merely said, "Don't look to either side. Keep your eyes focused on the crest *(mon)*[72] on the back of my *haori* and just keep coming!" It is related that Ginjibei then, by walking as he had been instructed, had no problem in keeping up. If we bear in mind the wholehearted and selfless state that one may enter at times, perhaps such a thing may not seem so impossible.

Visiting the Grand Shrines of Ise

The Founder made five pilgrimages to the Grand Shrines of Ise after the Direct Bestowal of Divine Mission. Together with the one he made at age 24, it makes a total of six. This was in an age when travel was much less convenient than today. The time required to make the sea and overland journey to and from Ise, on foot and by boat, was from thirty to forty days. For the people of Bizen Province to make the pilgrimage to Ise just once in a lifetime was ordinarily the most that could be hoped for at that time, since it was such a major journey.

The fact that Munetada made the trip six times shows how important it was. We can understand the great weight it carried for his religious beliefs.

Here is a summary of his pilgrimages to the Grand shrines of Ise, each taking about a month to complete, and his age at the time.

1st trip	3rd and 4th months of 1803	24 yrs.
2nd trip	3rd month of 1824	45 yrs.
3rd trip	4th month of 1831	52 yrs.
4th trip	3rd and 4th months of 1833	54 yrs.
5th trip	3rd and 4th months of 1835	56 yrs.
6th trip	3rd and 4th months of 1845	66 yrs.

Parts of his travel diaries from the second and fifth of these pilgrimages are still extant today.[73] They show that Munetada travelled from Okayama to Osaka either by boat or on foot. From Osaka to Kyoto he would go by boat up the Yodo River and then continue on foot from Kyoto by way of Kusatsu and Kameyama. After worshipping at Ise he would return on foot directly to Osaka and continue on home from there.

On the occasion of his 1824 pilgrimage, Munetada stopped in Kyoto to receive the approval of the Yoshida family for his succession to the position of deputy head priest *(negi)* of the Imamura Shrine. This made official the service he had already been giving ever since his revered father Kurozumi Muneshige had died. With the Yoshidas' sanction, the position was formalized. It was at this time that he took the name Kurozumi Munetada.

Travel expense at the time was about one *kan* 100 *mon* per day for two people, judging from the diaries. Total expense for two people for a pilgrimage trip of roughly 30 days would be about five or six *ryo*. A

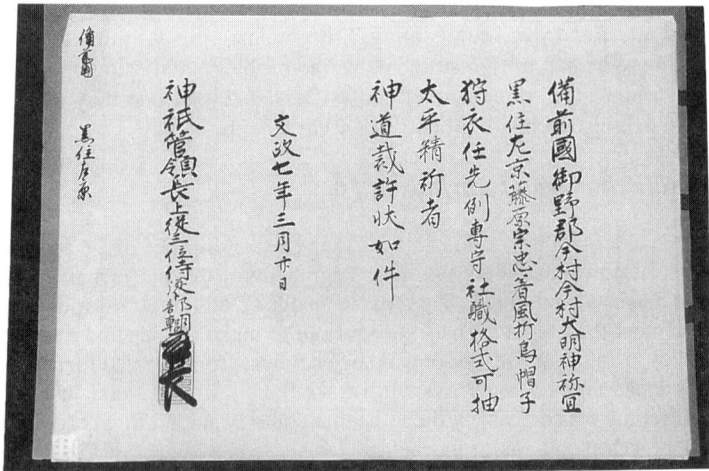

Fig. 6   Letter from the Yoshida office of Kyoto, officially appointing Kurozumi Munetada as priest with the rank of *negi*. The letter, sent in the third month of 1824, also authorizes the attire appropriate to the role. *Courtesy of Kurozumikyō.*

document from the Founder's 1833 pilgrimage shows that he was loaned five *ryo* by Beniya Yosuke.[74] This clearly states that the money was to cover travel expenses for the Ise pilgrimage. The equivalent of 5 *ryo* in today's money would be about 100,000 yen, based on the *ryo* as purchasing one *koku* (about five bushels) of rice.

Thus, the cost of the journey, in addition to the inconvenient transportation and other complexities of making travel arrangements, made the Ise pilgrimage quite difficult. That he went to the extent of borrowing the large amount of money necessary for the journey shows us again the deep meaning the Ise Shrine had for him and the eagerness of his faith.

As has already been related, Munetada once was asked by a priest of the Ise Shrine why he was offering all his prayers. His answer, "simply to pray for the good fortune of Amaterasu Ōmikami," shows the purpose he had for travelling from distant Bizen province, over many fields and mountains, on the Ise pilgrimage. In 1845, after returning from his last trip, he wrote in a letter:

> This Spring I journeyed to the Grand Shrine of Ise as planned, though there were a number of difficulties and it took longer than I expected. Please understand. However, in my worship at the Grand Shrine I was received in audience by Amaterasu and my joy knows no bounds. During this trip the Great Way has become especially clear to me.
>
> *Gobun* 178

A similar story concerns the time Munetada asked the high disciple Tokio Katsutarō (who became a member in 1844) to make the pilgrimage on his behalf. The Founder emphasized to him over and over, "Tokio, you must without fail hold an audience with the great Kami." This was during a New Year season. From this story and from the letter we can see how the Founder held audience with Amaterasu by means of the Ise pilgrimage. He prayed to receive her Good Fortune, in the continuous opening of divine grace as the Great Way expanded, and in the renewal of his faith. He often asked his disciples to go in his stead, and strongly encouraged his followers to make the journey for themselves.

It was the Founder's idea that those making the pilgrimage should wear an emblem with the design of the rising sun on it as a symbol of the Way. This came out of a concern that the followers be able to recognize each other at a glance among the masses of pilgrims.

This "badge" developed naturally into a symbol of the Great Way and eventually into an emblem of the Kurozumikyō organization. It became a custom to raise high the flag of the rising sun outside the various meeting places on the day of the monthly meeting. However, when the rising sun was adopted as the national flag of Japan at the beginning of the Meiji period, the character for "*kyō*" (teachings) was added in white inside the

red sun. The "circled *kyō*"[75] has become the official emblem of
Kurozumikyō.

Fig. 7   The "circled *kyō*," official emblem of
Kurozumikyō. *Courtesy of Kurozumikyō.*

The Thousand Day Retreat

All of life is religious practice, every moment of every hour, as long as one lives. This is what the Founder continually preached. In one sense it might then be difficult to see why he would continue to practice religious austerities, especially after such a great religious experience as the Direct Bestowal of Divine Mission.

On further reflection, however, we see that his continuing practice after that point has a special significance. We appreciate this partly by remembering that after that beginning point he was very active, not only in preaching the Way but also in fulfilling his social obligations as priest of the Imamura Shrine and as husband and father at home. We could call them "post-enlightenment religious austerities," a feature that is not often seen in other religions of the world.

We can understand another, deeper aspect of it, from a pledge *(shinmon)* to Amaterasu Ōmikami he wrote in 1824, shortly after returning from his second pilgrimage to the Grand Shrines of Ise, dated the fifth month of the year:

Divine Pledge

I offer up this pledge that I may once more be humbly favored to receive your proclamation.

By "once more" he meant a second time since the Bestowal of his Divine Mission was first experienced at age thirty-five. The date of this vow was exactly ten years after his enlightenment. It states his desire to be filled again with the deep emotion and grateful joy he had felt on the first occasion.

As already indicated, Munetada had come to believe that the slanders and obstacles the Way had encountered were the result of his own unworthiness. This made it all the more important that he reawaken the dauntless spirit within himself. There is no doubt that his decision to offer this vow could not have been easy. He also felt it necessary that as many people as possible in the world come to know the Way and be saved by it. This would only be possible if his innermost heart would be very humble and pure (*Gobun* 30). To cleanse his heart Munetada undertook a great many religious practices, and among them his thousand days of retreat deserves special mention.

This spiritual exercise is a period of nearly three full years, during which the one doing the retreat sleeps at night in a sacred place practicing all-night prayer.[76]

Throughout this time he fully carried out his duties as priest of the Imamura Shrine. In addition he conducted regular monthly meetings (on the second, seventh, 12th, 17th, 22nd, and 27th days of the month) as well as the recently established meeting in Okayama City, whose numbers had grown considerably. According to a letter written in 1826 to his disciple Ishio, he went out almost every night to a meeting. It was under these circumstances, on the 23rd of the seventh month in 1825, that the Founder began his thousand days of prayer. He conducted his retreat at the Imamura shrine, reciting the Great Purification Prayer nightly.[77] We may assume he was able to dedicate his whole heart to it. In that year he completed 155 days of prayer.

He continued in the same manner into 1826. In that year his oldest son, Munenobu, became afflicted with smallpox. (It was Munenobu, known in childhood as Sanokichi, who later was revered as the Second Patriarch.) Born in the sixth month of 1822, he was then five years old by Japanese reckoning. His illness became critical, and his mother as well as Ginjibei and others were extremely worried about him. Munetada, however, continued with his prayers. It troubled them, since it was, after all, his eldest son who was ill. The other children all were girls, and Munenobu was the sole and irreplaceable heir of the Kurozumi family. Going out every night while one's son was gravely ill was not good for appearances, and Ginjibei admonished Munetada for his behavior. But he just went on with his religious work and would not listen.

Then one day the illness worsened to the point that Munenobu was having trouble breathing. When this happened, Ginjibei rushed to the Imamura Shrine to inform the Founder of the crisis.

This time, after listening calmly, he took Ginjibei's right hand in both of his hands and performed *majinai*, blowing *yōki* into his palm. "Take this and return to give the same *majinai* to Munenobu for me. I'm sure that he will receive divine grace *(okage)*," he said. Then he sent Ginjibei off and did not go back himself. Ginjibei returned home without lowering his right hand and followed Munetada's instructions. He placed his hand on

Munenobu's chest and performed *majinai* by blowing *yōki* directly onto it. And, divine power brought a miracle so that Munenobu made a full recovery before long.

We must appreciate the devotion with which the Founder pursued his thousand days of retreat. This manifestation of his great faith in Amaterasu Omikami is indeed worthy of contemplation.

It appears his use of this practice deepened his ability to learn from life. We see this from a dream of his which he wrote about in a letter known as the story of the Snake Dream. He reported it this way:

> One night while in confinement in the Imamura Shrine I fell into a drowse and had a dream. In the dream I was sitting all alone when a swarm of snakes, large and small, came in countless numbers looking for a chance to torment me. The more I tried to brush them aside the more they came after me. They wrapped themselves around my arms and legs. They wrapped themselves around my neck. Everywhere, all the fields and mountains, were full of snakes. One large one flicked out its reddened tongue and tried to swallow me. I tried to escape, but there was nothing I could do.
>
> But when I looked carefully I could see that all I had always considered important — my beloved children and wife, as well as gold and silver and everything I had ever wanted — had all taken the form of snakes. And the largest one, their leader in their midst, I saw was my own body and flesh.
>
> At the moment when I was astonished and confused I suddenly remembered Amaterasu Ōmikami and I earnestly prayed to her, leaving everything in her hands. Then it was as though everything changed. Everything that had seemed fearful returned to its normal state. My wife and my children and my valuables became real treasures once again.
>
> If we become attached to our family and the things we value and lose our hearts, it all turns to snakes and serpents. But if we surrender everything to Amaterasu Ōmikami and accept all as gifts from her, then all those things will nurture our hearts and we can live abundantly. It is said that our daily perplexities show up in our dreaming, and I must have been in some kind of delusion at that time. However, I feel extreme gratitude for this kind of religious practice, giving nourishment for my heart's cultivation. I have told this experience to our followers, and they nodded their heads in agreement, sharing my sense of gratitude.
>
> *Gobun* 46

Using this dream, the Founder taught that attachment to external forms will bring suffering to our hearts. However, if we entrust everything to Kami and feel grateful for whatever we receive, then these same external forms can bring nourishment to our hearts.

Just the year before, his oldest daughter Koma had married a man by the name of Chayamachi Chojirō, but on the first day of the eighth month of this year he passed away suddenly in illness. We can imagine the deep shock and sadness the Founder experienced in losing the youthful husband of his beloved daughter. On the 16th day of the same month he wrote to Ishio:

Chayamachi Chojirō passed away on the first day of this month. It was indeed unexpected and caused much grief to me and to my family. We cannot really count on anything. However, we must accept it as another opportunity for religious practice. The Great Way is to accept all such events as practice. Let me say a little about the essence of my teaching.

Let us suppose there is a likely young man who grows up and meets a young woman and they get married. This makes two people. They then have five children, making seven, who eventually grow up and get married. This then makes a total of twelve people. If each of the children has five children each, a total of twenty-five grandchildren, then altogether we would have thirty-seven people.

But there is no guarantee that any of them will enjoy health and long life. The one who turns out to have responsibility for all thirty-seven will have many anxieties and worries. One might come down with smallpox or give birth painfully or fall victim to an epidemic. There might be a child who is bright and diligent, but others to our dismay might be dull and idle. These things and many others like them are apt to happen constantly. Days and nights would always be filled with worry.

This situation is referred to in Buddhism as "a burning house world," a life of suffering.[78] If one were to think of escaping by abandoning one's family and becoming a monk, carrying out religious practices all alone in the world, then one must remember there is not one in a thousand of these who becomes a person with deep comprehension. The point is that no one can manipulate his or her own heart according to their own wishes and desires. No matter how much one ponders the point, one must still live by means of one's own self. There is no other way.

However, what I am grateful for is that I am a child of Heaven and Earth and that a child born to me is also a child of Heaven and Earth. So, leaving all to the workings of Heaven and Earth, I accept its guidance. If we focus on true sincerity *(makoto)* as we have been taught, then favorable and unfavorable, birth and death, all become religious practice. We come to know everything as the will of Heaven.

By carrying out the will of Heaven there can be nothing that can cause us suffering in the least.

Gobun 47

During this year (1826) the Founder spent 319 nights in retreat in the Shrine followed by another 319 nights in 1827. In the first month of 1828 he spent five more nights in prayerful seclusion. Including the previously mentioned 155 days this made a total of 798 spent in religious retreat. This total is calculated from a "Memo of the Number of Days Spent in Confinement," which still exists. In another record, however, his *Gobun* 70, the Founder indicated that he was in continuous retreat from New Year's until the fourth month; and then from the 25th until the 29th day of the same month he spent the time in fasting as well. It was recorded later in the chronological record of the Founder's life that this final period marked the completion of his vow to spend a thousand nights in religious retreat.

Establishing the Seven Principles

The Founder's thousand-day retreat was a major turning point in his life, comparing in importance to his experience of the Direct Bestowal of Divine Mission in his 35th year, eleven years earlier. It extended over the four-year period between 1825 and 1828. As a result of it, the false rumors about him and his followers died down which had been spreading earlier, and the Way went on flourishing. During this fresh turning point, as a result of divine inspiration from Amaterasu Omikami, he also established the Seven Principles.

There was a need at this time to provide structure and guidance for the followers. From about the time the Founder was halfway through his retreat the Way began to grow greatly in numbers. On regular meeting days at his house, and at other places where meetings were held, there were throngs of worshipers and visitors in attendance. Sermons were given night after night. Even in such distant places as Wake-gun (about 35 kilometers away) and Oku-goori (about 20 kilometers) the Way was flourishing. With so many rapidly-growing groups being formed, the Seven Principles were needed as rules for the sake of good organization.

This very important statement was based on the Five Principles originally composed in his youth as his instructions to himself. The revised and expanded list was intended for his followers to use for their general guidance. It was the minimum to which they should commit themselves. The Founder wished to provide each follower with a copy, urging that they needed to put the rules to active use.

The Seven Principles are:

Daily Rules for the Whole Family

1. Born in the Land of the Gods, you shall not fail to cultivate faith.
2. You shall neither get angry nor worry.
3. You shall not give way to conceit nor look down upon others.
4. You shall not follow another's evil while increasing evil in your own heart.
5. You shall not slacken in the work of your house except in illness.
6. While pledged to the Way of Sincerity, you shall not lack sincerity in your own heart.
7. You must never stray from the spirit of gratitude.

The rules must never be
forgotten.

Standing before you
  others hold up mirrors
    as their own hearts
And there within you can see
  your own heart being
  reflected.[79]

These rules are intended for all members of Kurozumikyō families, even today, and if any follower neglects them, that person has lost ground spiritually, falling back in standing as a member.

The teachings may seem ordinary and unremarkable, but that is because they deal with everyday matters, and the soul of a religion is its ability to make the most of everyday life. No matter how profound an experience of insight *(satori)* or a teaching may be, if it is not expressed in everyday action its significance is lost. To put it another way, faith is practice *(gyō)*, something you do.

The first article is the nucleus of all seven. "Land of the Gods," or "Divine Land" *(Shinkoku)*, means the place blessed with the divine virtues, where the benevolence of Amaterasu Ōmikami is fostered. We who have been born to this world due to the goodness of Amaterasu Ōmikami, divine parent of the universe, should always be gratefully and faithfully minded

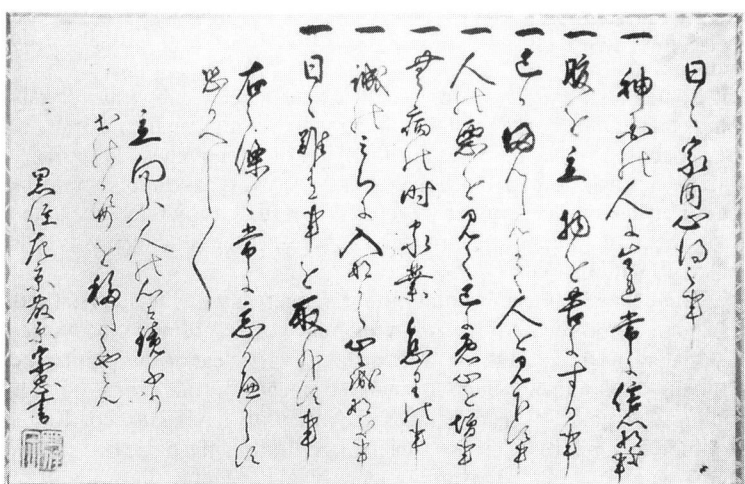

Fig. 8 The Seven Principles in the Founder's own calligraphy. The original hangs in the Founder's Memorial Hall. *Courtesy of Kurozumikyō.*

toward her. This is the essence of faith, and should be the foundation for everyone's living.

As to Article Two, keeping from getting angry and annoyed is the easiest thing for us humans to forget about. Even if we say we are not angry, often it is only that we are not letting our anger show. It is possible to be angry in our hearts but suppress it. This is mostly how we see people handling anger, or worry and distress. On the surface it might appear as a commendable kind of patience or perseverance, but actually it is another form of doing harm. This rule is not about patience; it is about reaching a point where we naturally do not even begin to get angry at all.

Consider some trouble or distress that is going on right now, in the present moment. What may actually be happening is our reflecting on the past with regret, saying, "I should have done that," or, "I could have said this." Or, maybe we are fretting about the future and grieving ourselves into perplexity over something that has not even happened yet. The former is an example of harm done by clinging to something in the past, and the latter is doing harm by needlessly worrying about the future. The Founder warned us to "stick to our basic idea" *(nen o tsugu)* and, not being distracted from the present, avoid both those tendencies so harmful to the heart.[80]

Article Three deals with conceit *(manshin)*. When everything is going along smoothly for us we may, without noticing it, be apt to start feeling self-satisfied, even pompous. Whenever we start feeling pompous we stop making progress. Not only do we stop making progress, but we begin to move backwards. This article teaches us that we should face everything that happens with humility, and be carefully attentive to all that we do and say.

Articles Four and Five, along with Article Three, deal with everyday things that come up, not with the intention of warning against matters of great evil, but rather pointing out that lack of attentiveness in ordinary actions can lead to bad consequences. Such everyday things are to be measured always not so much by reference to rules as by reference to the divine heart of Amaterasu Ōmikami, and whether the conduct involved is in accord with that heart.

Article Six clarifies this point further. Together with the others, it sets a standard for knowing if we are living our lives according to the wishes of Amaterasu Ōmikami or not. This article is very clear on this point. The ultimate standard is whether we have true sincerity in our hearts or if it is lacking. Article Seven concludes the list with having us not forget gratitude in our daily lives. The spirit of gratitude is the basic doctrine of Kurozumikyō. It is the most often mentioned concept in the scriptures.

Since the Seven Principles are the basis of all the teachings of Kurozumikyō, they are listed at the beginning of all its texts and scriptures.

Even today when a person becomes a follower *(michizure),* offering a pledge to the spirit of the Founder, he or she must first of all vow to observe the Seven Articles strictly.

The religious practice of the Founder, then, was never some kind of asceticism or self-mortification. It was just doing the things you normally do in daily activities in a serious way, with an attitude of faith. Members of Kurozumikyō follow the way he established, completely confident that the path of everyday living is in fact the Way to become kami.[81] His practice did not involve any kind of strange or unusual exertions.

Finally, the religious practice he followed after his enlightenment is based on his concept that "to become kami is to become human." Kami and the human are one and inseparable. The Founder experienced this for himself as he deepened his life through these religious practices. The Seven Principles need to be studied and followed in order to gain the same realization. This is the commitment of members of Kurozumikyō.

Sermons as Words from Heaven

The Founder said of his sermons that they were words from Heaven *(Tengen).* He believed the words he spoke as he preached were of him but not his. They were the words of Amaterasu Ōmikami speaking through him.

One time at a meeting held in the home of Rokuzaemon, the roof-tile-maker, the Founder said to the people gathered,

> Today on my way here I prayed to the setting sun and I feel such thankfulness, such thankfulness. Feeling such thankfulness, nothing else comes to mind. So tonight I will end here. Ah, such thankfulness, thank you. Thank you very much.

And, so saying, he came down from the platform. It is also recorded that there were a number of sick people in attendance on this occasion and they all received blessing and help *(Tales of the Founder* 63).

So there were times when the Founder said hardly anything at all except, "thank you, thank you,"[82] and stepped down from the speaker's seat. At one such presentation a follower came up to the Founder afterwards and said,

> A great number of followers have come here, some of them from great distances, in the joyful hope of hearing a sermon on the Way. Hearing you merely say, "thank you" and depart is disappointing to them. Also, there are those who do not understand the thought behind the Way and therefore cannot enter the path. I feel that these people need things more fully explained to them.

Hearing this the Founder was most delighted, and replied:

> You have brought up a very good point. I appreciate your devotedness very
> much. But when it comes to sermons on the Way, I always explain that they
> are the words of Amaterasu Ōmikami. It would be a mistake to think of them
> as coming from the human intellect. Since all I do is done through leaving
> it to the will of Heaven, the followers will be blessed with a simple "thank
> you, thank you." When Heaven's time comes, the whole country of Japan
> will be fully grateful.

The Founder also said of these "words from Heaven" that he gave them
"just as they float up" *(ukabi no mama)*. He did not use notes or an outline
when he gave sermons. He also warned his followers against too much
structure when they spoke, saying they should not become mere "sermon
carpenters." The essence of his preaching was free of all rules of
composition. He just let his words rise up unhampered and spontaneous.
In the *Short Biography* the Founder is quoted as saying,

> When I lecture I do not rely at all on any sort of written materials. Since in
> each moment I speak I am following the will of Heaven, I may on occasion
> say "east" after saying "west" or, after saying something is so, right after that
> talk about it as not being so. But, since the inner heart is the same each time,
> just listening is the most important thing. People with learning[83] should
> discard their learning; even those people who are wise or virtuous should put
> aside their standards of measuring that. All need to get themselves out of
> an egoistic attitude and merely listen single-heartedly without attachment to
> the words that are said. Without that state of mind no one can understand
> anything I say.

Of course, the sermons or words that just floated up were not haphazard
or nonsense. They actually were the words of Amaterasu Ōmikami,
coming by way of his inner spirit *(bunshin)* that had become so attentive
to the inner presence of Amaterasu due to the Direct Bestowal of Divine
Mission he had experienced, and to the religious practices he followed
after that enlightenment. For this reason his sermons were not something
he prepared in advance, nor were they given with the intention of
explaining one thing or another.

This means, of course, that the Founder did not include in his sermons
any vestige of self-will or biased feelings. It is for this reason that his
sermons are referred to as "words of Heaven" *(tengen)*, "will of Heaven"
(tenmei), or "something alive" *(ikimono)*.

This can be observed also in his letters. While writing letters he would on occasion go into a state of nothingness (*mushin*, "no-mind") and write in the same spirit as when he preached. He once wrote,

> I am writing about the Way in the same state of feeling as when I lecture. In this state of nothingness, I do not know what it is I will write. I feel these writings are something alive, and ask that you read these words with this in mind.
>
> *Gobun* 136

Other letters also describe the state that he entered when he wrote on the Way. In *Gobun* 140 he refers to having written in a state of freedom from thought *(munen)*. In another he writes,

> The other day I wanted to write down what I had said in a sermon, and as I started to write things began to float up and the letter soon became the same as a sermon. I truly entered the state of nothingness as the letter was written. I wish you to read it in the same spirit.
>
> *Gobun* 144

We can see the same point made in a number of his letters. The Founder in giving lectures had the ability to leave his consciousness of himself behind, and then, unattached to the thoughts and ideas he was expressing, let the words spoken this way, originating with Amaterasu herself, be living and active, invigorating others and saving them from their illness and trouble.

Achievements of the Tempō Era (1830-1844)

Beginning with the third month of 1830 the Founder gave much attention to the religious practice called "visiting 100 shrines." As the *Chronology of The Founder's Life* tells us, from this time until the eleventh month of 1832 he paid his respects at 100 different Shinto shrines per month for this period of 33 months, as a religious discipline. It seems that he no longer found enough satisfaction in his daily five-shrines' visitation. We see again his unquenchable zest for religious practice.

Also, during this time he carried out a long fast because of a serious illness. This began on the seventh day of the seventh month of 1832. Though he was on the brink of death, he still spoke at the regularly scheduled meetings at his house. It has been reported that on these occasions he was actually carried, bedclothes and all, to the speaker's seat by several of his followers. Once he was seated he changed drastically, and in a renewed vigorous state he spoke with a voice like thunder. It is apparent how seriously he took these sermons and how strong his faith was. On the second day of the eighth month he had completely recovered. It has also been recorded that Ginjibei made a pilgrimage to the Ise Shrine in his behalf on the occasion of this illness.

In the third month of 1833 the Founder petitioned the Yoshida family in Kyoto that his parents be accorded the status of kami. The request was granted, with his father being given the sacred name of Iwane Reijin, and his mother, Eiju Reijin. Their spirits were enshrined under these names at the Omoto family shrine in Okayama. When Kurozumikyō headquarters was moved to Shintozan in 1974, their shrines were moved to the back garden of the new official residence of Chief Patriarch Muneharu Kurozumi, and they are worshiped there today.

On the 23rd day of the sixth month of this year the Founder received a letter from Ishio inviting him to the residence of the retired Daimyō of the Ikeda clan, Ikeda Narimasa, to pray for his recovery from illness. At the close of his letter Ishio adds,

> The time of the opening of the good fortune of Amaterasu Ōmikami has come! Indeed, I am so grateful.

This was a real shout of joy that the Way of Amaterasu Ōmikami and the virtues of the Founder had reached the ears of the former clan chieftain. The Daimyō himself had requested these prayers for his recovery.

A number of other highly placed members of the clan became followers. A document compiled in 1834, listing the names and addresses of followers of the Way, includes these names: Ikeda Tamba (head of the Ikusaka branch of the Ikeda family, income listed as 15,000 *koku* of rice), Ikeda Nakatsukasa Shofu (adopted son of Ikeda Tamba), as well as Ikeda Izumo (chief retainer of the Ikeda household whose income was 30,000 *koku* of rice.)

In the second month of 1835 the Founder's second daughter Naka married Sakurai Kimata. His family had for generations served as priests at the Kibitsugu, the most important Shinto shrine in the Kibi area west of Okayama.[84] Sakurai became a follower in 1841, and later departed for the eastern part of present day Tottori Prefecture to do missionary work. Through great diligence he accomplished much wonderful work there, and later came to be considered its major pioneer in preaching the Way. In 1849, however, he died while visiting there for the second time.

Also in 1835, the Founder's son Munenobu fell gravely ill just as he turned 14. Munetada had been planning a trip to preach in the Mimasaka area, located in today's northern Okayama Prefecture. The Founder's family and followers tried to dissuade him from going away. But he said, as he was leaving, that since he was involved with the work of Kami and many people would receive the blessing of healing, surely his own child would not be an exception. It is reported that after he had been gone about a week Munenobu showed a remarkable recovery (*Tales of the Founder* 32).

It is plain to see that the Founder had become a person of remarkable strength of character. In 1836, for instance, on the 15th day of the sixth month, he wrote out the following prayer:

Divine Pledge

To all kami of Heaven and Earth and to the eight million kami:

I offer up this prayer. Though I am so lacking in virtue, I have graciously and freely been given instruction from Heaven *(Shizen tenmei o uke).* From that time on I have never disobeyed any instruction from Heaven, and certainly none of the laws of my country.

Yet now, though our people have sincerely followed the Way for years, I have heard that some officials look upon us with doubt and we are dismayed. In humble solicitation, and fully confident of our uprightness in the Way, I pray that any doubts the ruler or his retainers may have be cleared away. It is for this I most humbly and earnestly pray to Amaterasu Ōmikami. In awe and sincerity.

15th day of the sixth
month of the seventh
year of Tempō (1836)
Kurozumi Sakyo Fujiwara
no Munetada.

Clearly, in writing that he had received "instruction from Heaven," the Founder was referring to his enlightenment experience at age 35 when he was granted his mission from Heaven. We can also see his devoted striving to carry on this work according to the strict standards that he had set for himself. While we don't know what sort of "doubt" the officials had, we see that the Founder handled the matter in a poised and honorable way.

Another incident in these years also shows the kind of person the Founder was. On the 23rd day of the third month of 1838 an Okayama samurai by the name of Matsuo Chozaburō, inflamed with drink after attending a cherry blossom viewing party not far from the Okayama castle, turned his sword on a number of people and ended up injuring 23 or 24 of them. As he passed by the Nakano-chō gate of the castle, Matsuo raised his sword against the Founder. But he calmly warned the man, saying "consider where it is that you are doing this." On hearing this, Matsuo quieted down, put away his sword, bowed to Munetada courteously, and departed.

The Founder knew, as the other man was also supposed to know, that there was a serious penalty on any samurai unsheathing a sword there in the neighborhood of the castle. The penalty was *seppuku,* death by his own sword. It would also mean the end of Matsuo's family line since they too would be punished. It was these consequences of what the man was doing that concerned the Founder. Thus, while disregarding his own safety completely, he needed to say only one simple thing in order to bring the drunken man to his senses (*Tales of the Founder* 70).

Letters Written During the Tempō Era

During the years 1840 to 1842 there were a number of Okayama samurai who, one after another, became followers of the Way. The list includes Taguchi Aizo (income of 200 *koku*), Yamada Yataro (300 *koku*), and Ozeki Jyogoro (400 *koku*). They were samurai of high rank and income and they were also men of learning and culture. Under the alternating residency system required of them at the time, they accompanied the Bizen clan lord in serving in the Shogun's headquarters at Edo, and thus they received a number of letters from the Founder.

These letters are comparable in subject matter to the ones he had written earlier to Ishio. Many of them are invaluable documents about the Way, giving us insight into the heart of the Founder's teaching.

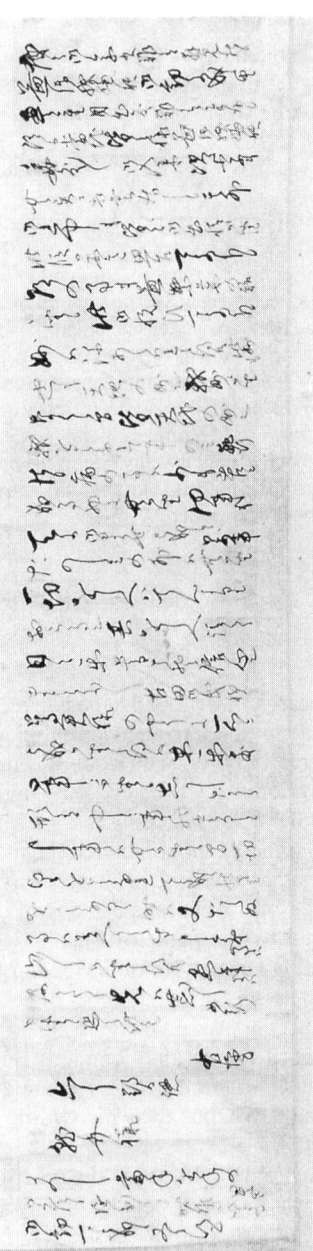

Fig. 9   This one of the Founder's letters to Ishio Kensuke. *Courtesy of Kurozumikyō.*

In one letter, dated the third month of 1842, probably written to Ozeki, he writes:

> As we had promised each other before your departure. I will be meeting with you at *nippai* each and every morning. Please do not forget your promise. The Way is nothing other than Roundness." A poem says it this way:

> Inside of Roundness
>   a person possessing
>   a roundness of heart
> Will never know of limits
>   here within the Roundness.

> This is just what abiding life is about. No limits should be set on anything at all. Within the divine roundness there is no aging. Gratitude to the Roundness must never be forgotten, even for a moment. Joy, happiness, trouble, and sorrow are all determined by how our hearts accept what happens. Gloom has no place with a faith in Amaterasu Ōmikami. Let us never be negligent of these points, even for a moment. Always be alert and attentive.

Gobun 136

In the same month he wrote to Taguchi Aizo:

> As I previously told you I would, I am observing *nippai* with the thought in mind each and every morning that I am enjoying it with you. So, please do not be negligent.
>   The Great Way is indeed something brimming with gratitude. To stay always within the Roundness as we live our lives day after day, to live on always with gratitude and joy, is to know that this faithful life is just the same thing as the heart's impulse of Amaterasu Ōmikami. So, please do not ever forget to cultivate your heart by means of the Seven Principles.

> Ah, such joyfulness
>   here in the delightfulness
>   of this world of ours,
> Who can call this present world[86]
>   merely a path of suffering?

> Once we open our hearts we do not experience worry or trouble at all. Everything is experienced with joy and gratitude. We can choose to open our hearts or to close them, and our choosing is then done with the poise that makes all the difference.

Gobun 137

There are numerous letters such as these in which the Founder explained the Way in straightforward and steadfast fashion. He especially encouraged the performance of *nippai* in these messages, urging strict daily observance. When he wrote that he would be meeting the others each and every morning at the *nippai* service he was saying that he would be "meeting" Ozeki and Taguchi, but of course these men would also be striving to meet the Founder while separately performing their own services. They would do it in a shared belief and desire to be together with Munetada. Of course, this idea did not include only the two samurai mentioned. All the followers of the Way performed the *nippai* service with the intention of "meeting" with the Founder.

In a poem probably composed in the second month of 1837 and given as a parting gift to Goshi Mozaemon, an Okayama samurai being sent to Edo for duty, the Founder said:

> As you now depart
>   To the ends of the Eastlands
>   We will still remain
> In the same heart of Kami,
>   The same True Sincerity.
>   To Goshi Mozaemon
>   From Kurozumi Sakyo.[87]
>   *O-uta* 104

This poem shows the Founder's idea that through the practice of *nippai*, in which all focused in separate places upon Amaterasu Ōmikami, an interchange would occur between each of the inner spirits *(bunshin)* of the men.

In 1842 the Founder wrote to Ozeki:

> The Way has in it a full abundance of divine blessing. Coming from Amaterasu Ōmikami, it can only be full and lack nothing. We must be sure that our inner spirits keep the intended roundness and not be missing something. When people become negligent in vital essence *(yōki)*, then gloom *(inki)* grows stronger. When gloom wins, the result is impurity *(kegare).*[88] This inner impurity forms as a withering of essence *(ki)*. It dries up the great sun essence *(dai yōki)* within. If, as we spend our days, we only would accept all things with gratitude, there would be nothing but the feelings of gratitude.

> If for all things
>   we possess a gratitude
>   as we live our lives,
> Then the things we have to face
>   will bring us more gratitude.

> If we receive both what we prefer and what appears to us as unfavorable with gratitude, then we will come to live with gratitude at all times and in all ways.
>   *Gobun* 143

When the Founder writes in this letter that the Way *(michi)* is full *(michiru)*, he is using the sound of these two words to help explain the meaning. By *"michiru"* (full or be filled) he is saying that the vital essence of Amaterasu Ōmikami fills up our bodies. He also explains that *yōki* and *inki* are mutually related. When we are feeling vital then gloominess disappears, but when we are feeling gloomy our vital energy grows quite thin. From the ancient past *kegare* has been explained in various ways, but, in essence, it is a drying up of our *yōki* or energy of the sun. This in turn causes distress, suffering, illness, and poverty. We must prevent our *yōki* from drying up. It all really comes down to living our lives in gratitude for all things.

The Founder taught us some very specific methods for bringing this vital essence into our lives. *Yōki shugyō*, the religious practice of vital energies, is closely related to *nippai shugyō*, the religious practice of daily sun worship. The two should be done together as a single practice. In doing it this way, when we take a strong in-breath while facing the rising sun it is not a merely a case of breathing deeply the morning air. It is receiving the great living energy of the Sun of all of Heaven and Earth. It is receiving divine virtue itself.

The method used is one of taking in the atmosphere, not into the chest and the lungs, but into the abdomen and the digestive system. Physically, this practice revitalizes the body and restores its strength. But the real aim is to provide a religious discipline through which we can become one with the Universe, cultivating the vital breath *(ki)* of all of Heaven and Earth, and thus attain inner peace. It is a religious practice by which we can find inner peace in a state of selflessness *(muga)*. In this state of spirit there surges up from the depths of our bodies the feeling of true gratitude. By it we are recreated constantly. The Founder wrote:

> Day after day
>   We face the morning sun
>   aware in our hearts
> That our lives are limitless,
>   A feeling of such joy.
>   *O-uta* 158

He went on to explain this condition as "abiding life." In this "living through" *(ikidōshi)*, our lives gain oneness as Heaven and Earth come together as one in each single moment of life, and the Way is limitless. A person who is living in wonder and joy, having gotten rid of gloom, is living in oneness with all of Heaven and Earth. This is the abiding life of a person who truly has faith. It is the ultimate experience that everyone should attain. To come up to this level and live such a life or not is left up to us completely; it is fully our own decision, made by our own hearts.

We can open or we can close these hearts of ours. The Founder encouraged us to choose what is for our benefit.

The beginning of his own faith was firmly established with his experience of the Bestowal of Divine Mission and it remained unchanged the rest of his life. However, his faith increased in depth with increasing age, both through his life experiences as they accumulated and through the effect of the religious practices he carried out after reaching enlightenment. Indeed, without question he savored in later years the increasing subtlety and richness of a deepening faith. It was his religious practices after enlightenment that provided this richness.

It is because of the insight they give into this development that the letters written by the Founder during the Tempō period are so full of interest to us. Among them, the ones addressed to Ichimori Hikorokuro (an Okayama samurai with an income of 120 *koku* of rice) stand apart as quite unique in content.

Ichimori became a believer in 1824. Born in 1807, he was still quite young. Having lost his father early and having a mother who became a follower in 1822, Ichimori appears to have received a bit of fatherly advice along with the spiritual guidance of the Founder. A letter of the tenth month of 1835 reads:

> The other day I heard from your mother, who is taking care of things here in Okayama while you are gone, that you have been much affected by the death of your cousin and don't feel like doing much of anything. This is understandable, but there is nothing you can do about what has happened. Now the time for purification has come, for moving away from it. To continue to think longingly about those who will not return is called attachment or persistence. It does not do any good for those who have left us and it is not any good for you. It is better to come out of your mood, and offer prayers for the benefit of the deceased.[89]

Gobun 88

In another letter of this period, in the 11th month of 1839, Munetada writes:

> I have often said that there is one thing which is basic amidst the events of our lives that takes so many shapes: to take good care of our inner spirit. Doing this puts us on the path of becoming kami. In this world as we have it, facing evil is how we come to do that. Everything that happens comes from Kami, but as we experience it, it is relative, and can either be right *(zen)* or wrong *(aku)*.
>
> So, the evil we experience is our own state of delusion and doubt, and to awaken from delusion is what we must do. Therefore, whenever we see evil it is actually an opportunity to increase the good that much the more. Evil and good come together as one in the pure practice of the Way.

Gobun 126

In the sixth month of 1843 the Founder further wrote:

> As I explained to you directly the other day, most things that happen to us every day are not our own doing, and when we occupy ourselves too much with them they end up seeming meaningless and dreary. We take them too much to heart because we are under the impression that these little bodies are our own. This is the point where religious practice becomes necessary. If we practice considering that our bodies are not our own but are created by Kami and belong to Amaterasu, and to rulers and parents, then our hearts will be free of worry about small things.
>
> *Gobun* 159

When we read such letters to Ichimori carefully, we are struck with the considerable difference in content from the letters written to Ozeki and Taguchi. To Ichimori Munetada gave guidance related to daily and family matters as well as to those matters related to occupational service and duty.

The Secret of All Disciplines and All Teachings

Every possible teaching and form of skill[90] has its source in the Way, given to us by the parental deity of the universe. The Founder was able to give expression to the words of Amaterasu Ōmikami naturally while in a totally selfless state, completely free of all self-interest, having abandoned both wisdom and prudence. What the Founder transmitted to us out of that state of mind are heavenly words and divine teachings containing all mysteries. They are the secrets of the Way, providing the basis of all disciplines and religious practices.

The Founder wrote:

> The other day I was speaking to a Shinto priest, a man who had forty years of experience in religious practices. He had a number of questions on points he had studied for a long time. When I answered them directly and clearly, he was much impressed and moved by what I said. It was an opportunity for me to teach him the secrets of those disciplines. This was not limited to followers of Shinto, for the same thing occurred with some followers of Buddhism.
>
> *Gobun* 39

Also, the *Short Biography* says:

> People who had practiced various arts and disciplines, but who found it hard to get the knack of their professions, were awakened by Munetada to the secrets of those arts. Similarly, people devoted to a particular religious practice or faith, whether Shinto, Confucianism, or Buddhism, have through Munetada's assistance gained a deep awareness of the underlying meaning of those paths.

What this is saying is that followers of Shinto have gained deeper understanding of their own Shinto, and Buddhists have, in the same way, become able to grasp the deeper mysteries of their faith. In fact, both Shinto and Buddhist priests became followers of the Way in great numbers. Examples of these Shinto priests are: Fujiwara Chitose of the Imamura Shrine, who became a member in 1824; Yuasa Satsuma, who entered in 1845; and Nonoue Tatewaki, who became a follower in 1849.

As for Buddhist priests, there were such people as Taikan, priest of the Tendai sect who entered the way in 1845, and Genkei and Genpo of the Bukkyoji Temple, initiated in 1849.

However, it was not only members of the religious community who were initiated into the mysteries of their own practice. The Founder also taught the inner secret of any discipline to its practitioners.

The afore-mentioned Ichimori Hikorokuro had been trained from childhood in the discipline of horsemanship. He was quite self-confident about his abilities, but on one occasion he heard the Founder speaking on the topic of "initiation into the secrets of all disciplines." Ichimori went up to him and asked to be initiated into the secrets of horsemanship. He replied, "First show me how you ride." Ichimori immediately mounted his horse and rode to let him see his style. After observing this display of horsemanship the Founder merely commented that he rode well. Not satisfied with that response, Ichimori requested to be told something more. The Founder then said, "You should not ride the horse," and composed the following poem:

> Amaterasu's
> Heart and a person's heart
>   are one and the same;
> Do not let loose the reins
>   whenever you're on horseback.

As the story goes, Ichimori was profoundly illuminated on hearing this. He realized the connection between the Founder's words and an important point of horsemanship. It is a point also expressed in the saying, "No rider above the saddle; no horse under the saddle." He grasped the mystery of the oneness of horse and man, based on the oneness of Amaterasu and man (*Tales of the Founder* suppl. 11).

This insight applies also to other kinds of skill. In Okayama there was a famous master of swordsmanship *(kendō)* by the name of Abe Ugenji, reputedly one of the four best swordsmen in Japan at the time. In a bout with another leading swordsman, Abe found that he just could not win. Unable to come up with a solution to his problem on his own, he decided to seek the advice of the Founder. After listening to the man's story he merely said one thing: "Abe-san, you shouldn't try to win."

Hearing this, Abe suddenly understood completely and gave most humble heartfelt thanks. The Founder's advice made him realize that his thoughts had been fixed first of all on winning. His mind was set on the thought that he held such a high position as fencing instructor to the ruling clan of Bizen, and that if he were to lose he would bring shame to himself. This worry so dominated his mind before a bout that his muscles became tight, and the considerable skill he did possess was lost. It was for this reason that he was unable to win. However, with the Founder's one comment, the pressure was lifted from Abe's heart. When he next faced the same swordsman, his opponent flung aside his bamboo sword and announced his surrender. The defeated man even went on to reproach Abe for just toying with him in the previous bouts, so impressed was he now by his ability. Anyway, this is the story of how Abe deepened his understanding of swordsmanship.

In much the same way there is a story told about a man by the name of Katayama who was lancing master to the Okayama clan. He also received instruction from the Founder on secrets of the spear. And, a potter by the name of Kimura Seiemon received help from the Founder in his profession of making Bizen pottery. Many people from various disciplines and callings received important lessons or blessings from him. The sick, upon hearing the Founder's teachings on the Way, had their hearts opened to the light and were healed. The poor, upon accepting the teachings, were opened to a change of fortune. Merchants prospered in business. The same truth of the Way applies in every case.

The advice Munetada was able to give to these skilled people of many kinds shows the results of all the spiritual progress he made during these years of deepening aspiration and growing inner purity.

Chapter Six

Forming the Religious Organization

In the closing decade of Munetada's life he gave the growing fellowship a sound organizational basis. His disciples and followers contributed strongly to this development, supporting the opening of the Way that continued after his death. Near the end of his life the death of his wife was a severe loss, and coming to terms with it was a step in the further deepening of his faith. He faced his own physical end, not long thereafter, in a spirit of calm acceptance. In the end, those who followed him as disciples and members were not left alone, but had his promise to be with them along the Way.

A Rapid Increase in Followers

The process of establishment began in 1841 when Munetada took steps to devote himself to fulltime leadership. On the 25th day of the second month, at the age of 62, he passed on his position as head of the family to his 20-year old son, Munenobu. Then, in 1843, he also turned over to his son his office as deputy priest of the Imamura Shrine. For some time he had wished to be free of this position. His priestly duties had restricted the time he had available, and the nature of the position had limited the kinds of things he could do. Now, however, free of that, he was able to engage himself singlemindedly in promoting the Great Way.

A rapid rise in the number of disciples *(monjin)* beginning about that time is clear from a look at the *Register of Disciples*. The growth in the number of people offering written vows, recorded there, is an indication of the increase in followers *(michizure)* that also was occurring. By one estimate, only about one percent of those regarded as followers committed themselves by making the pledge. The number of disciples was about 1150 by 1850 when Munetada died, and the number of followers was far greater than that. The overall increase, occurring across social classes from townspeople up to samurai, undoubtedly is due to Munetada's newly acquired freedom and full attention.

Among the most prominent new disciples of the time are: Miyata Shō, a Confucian scholar who entered the Way in 1843; Hoshijima Miya (1816-1857), mother of Hoshijima Ryōhei; Hoshijima Ryōhei himself (1835-1879), one of the six high disciples; and Hachiya Shunzō, a physician. Some who became members between 1844 and 1848 are: Hiramatsu Yoheiji, an Okayama clan retainer; Nakayama Tsunejirō (1802-1859), village head in Ogashima in Oku County; Tokio Katsutarō (1817-1862), one of the four high disciples; Jikihara Sukekuro, from the Mimasaka area and author of the *Memorandum of the Founder's Sermons and Lectures,* who entered in 1844; Morishita Keitan (1824-1891), one of the six high disciples; Fujita Shosuke (1816-1857), chief retainer of Ikeda Hyōgo of the Okayama clan; Morikane Tamezo (1821-1880), who entered in 1847; and others.

The Regulations of 1846

Up to this time the Seven Principles had served as criteria of faith which the followers would promise Munetada to abide by. Now, however, the growing size of the religious body made it necessary to draw up some kind of code. Thus, in the fourth month of 1846 the Six Regulations were drafted by an inner group of disciples *(montei gyōji)* designated for that purpose, and published under the name of one of them whom they had selected to act in their behalf. Later the others signed it as well, so that the regulations were published with their joint approval.

During the time this code was being established the group surrounding Munetada, at first spontaneously formed, became both in name and in fact, the Kurozumi *Kyōdan.*[91]

Here is a summary of the first three regulations:

1. Since the way of Amaterasu Ōmikami is such an important thing to us, we ask those who newly enter upon it to keep it ever in mind earnestly. If anyone, even those who have been followers for years, were to continue just out of habit, and just listen to sermons in a light and carefree way, it would be contrary to the Great Way. Rather, we should devote ourselves with sincere attention and cultivate our hearts in ever-deepening humility.

2. Substituting for the Founder by giving sermons in his place is a very important responsibility. No one should do this unless he has approved it in advance. Sometimes the Founder asks someone to give an opening lecture. But even if someone were to do this on one occasion, that does not include permission to substitute for him on later occasions.

3. Even those who have offered up their pledge and are very firm believers must not go out to other places and give sermons or perform *majinai* without the Founder's direction to do so. Such action is an offence against Amaterasu Ōmikami and out of a sense of awe is always to be prohibited.

These first three regulations emphasize the value and joy of the Way of Amaterasu Ōmikami. Both new followers and old must always renew their hearts, fully devoting themselves to their faith and listening to sermons with full attention.

Secondly, to insure an individual's preparedness for preaching and to prevent the disorderly practice of *majinai*, permission from Munetada is necessary in order to do them. This is the main concern of the document. The disciples who prepared it no doubt based it on the "Document Concerning Missionary Activity" of 1816.

The draft was given to Munetada, who made corrections and approved it, and it was then publicized under the names of the disciples and their representatives. The regulations were not printed, but they were carefully hand-copied and carried around by those who went out on teaching missions.

Once, while in Nagasaki doing missionary work, this writer saw a document entitled "Rules for the Lecture Hall,"[92] written sometime between 1854 and 1859 by one of the Founder's direct disciples, who had been invited there while preaching in Yanagawa (in present-day Fukuoka prefecture). The document consisted of a set of regulations concerning the establishment of the lecture hall in Nagasaki. The contents of the first three of them were exactly that of the first three of the Regulations of 1846. In an age lacking in transportation and communication facilities, it is amazing that these rules had circulated so far in such a short time. It would seem they were better disseminated than might be imagined.

There is another point worth pondering. For a founder of a religious group to approve setting up an organizational code for its members was something rare prior to the Meiji Period, though it is commonly seen today. Although many kinds of religious groups form, many of them shy away from doing that, or they just let matters run their course. However, in Kurozumikyō's case, the Founder was pleased at the thought of establishing an organization. He strongly wished his followers to organize so they would have better opportunities for self-cultivation and spiritual improvement, and as a result be blessed by all the divine virtues. One might say it is a necessary step for a religion with a broad and inclusive viewpoint to take.[93]

The spirit of the "Regulations of 1846" guided the subsequent development of the organization. The "Omoto House Regulations," drafted in 1860 to govern the wider Kurozumi "household" *(ie)* after the Founder had passed away, as well as today's "Kurozumikyō Church Regulations,"[94] are written in similar fashion.

Construction of His Residence

In 1846, soon after the regulations were enacted, discussions began about putting up a new building to serve as a residence and center for the Founder's work. Due to the great increase in followers, his home could no longer accommodate everyone on meeting days. The number of people put to inconvenience must have been great.

Many opinions were offered as to the style the new structure should have. Since it was to serve two purposes, both as a residence and as a meeting place, there were questions as to whether or not two structures should be built; or, if only one, whether the architecture should be that of a samurai home (since that was the Kurozumis' formal status) or a meeting hall. Finally a compromise was reached and a "Prospectus for Construction" was set forth by the disciples in the eleventh month.

According to this document, the Founder had on several previous occasions been advised to enlarge his home in order to accommodate the greater number of people attending meetings as a result of the recent blossoming of the Way. He had, however, refused. But the number of followers continued to increase, with those coming from far away being inconvenienced the most. So, when he was again advised to build, he gave his consent and construction began.

However, Munetada did not have the financial means to pay for this work. He had not expected to have to rebuild his home and had not provided for it. After discussion, the disciples agreed on a suggestion by several of them to ask for donations. They then issued an announcement to the followers expressing a desire for their cooperation, but stipulating that people should give only what they could afford and stating that the records would list only the names of the donors and not the amount given. The greatest care and consideration was put into this solicitation to make sure that no one would feel forced to take on an undue burden.

The building was completed in 1848 and is today preserved as the Founder's Memorial Hall *(Kyōso Kinenkan)*. For the last two years of his life, Munetada used it to live in as well as conduct his work, preaching there and giving *majinai*. The entire building, except for parts requiring skilled labor, was constructed by followers, who volunteered their labor gladly, down to carrying the dirt.

Distress in a Boat off Kogushi Village

On the eighth day of the third month of 1846, an unusual event occurred. While traveling by boat in Kojima bay, enroute to Shodo Island in the Seto

Inland Sea, the Founder experienced sudden and great danger. As the boat was passing the village of Kogushi, the seas suddenly became very rough so that nearby boats began capsizing. The situation became critical and there was nothing the boatman could do about it. He was about to warn the passengers to prepare for the worst. Munetada quietly took out a piece of paper from the pocket of his kimono sleeve and wrote this poem:

> Oh, god of the sea
>> Your angry billows and waves
>>> ought to be at peace;
> A knower of the True Sun
>> is aboard this very boat.[95]

It is said that when he tossed the poem into the roaring sea the winds and the waves became still.

The anecdote, referred to as the "Distress in a Boat off Kogushi," is recorded in the diary of Ito Sadasaburō of Togo-cho in present-day Tottori Prefecture, who was a passenger on a nearby boat at the time. Other passengers on the boat also repeated the story, so that it came to be quite well known.[96]

Fig. 10   This is the house built for the Founder, completed in 1848. It is adjacent to the Munetada Shrine in Omoto, and serves today as a museum. It is known as the Founder's Memorial Hall *(Kyōso Kinenkan). Courtesy of Kurozumikyō.*

Fig. 11   This room inside the Memorial Hall was the Founder's principal place
of work during the last two years of his life. The ritual streamers *(gohei)* and sacred
rope *(shimenawa)* above the alcove *(tokonoma)* show the reverence in which he is
held. The Takeda portrait hangs in the *tokonoma*. *Courtesy of Kurozumikyō.*

The Register of Disciples

The *Register of Disciples* is an important document that demonstrates the
connection between the Founder and his most important followers. In the
summer of 1847 the High Disciple Tokio Katsutarō wrote a preface for it
showing this. As stated previously (Chapter Four), the register begins in
1815 with the first disciple, Ono Eizaburō, and continues in chronological
order up to 1850, listing the names and addresses of the disciples as they
joined. With the names added after 1847 it contained nearly 1150 entries.
Unfortunately, the original text was water-damaged twice during floods in
the Meiji Period, causing the glue binding the book to loosen. It is believed
that some pages may have become separated and lost, so the *Register*
which remains today is, more correctly, what still survives of the text.
    The preface reads:

> People of ancient times said truly that the movements of the sun, rising daily
> in the east and setting in the west, never cease. But in our own times, Shinto
> beliefs have been waning in our land, while the light of Confucianism and

Buddhism has been flourishing. Now, however, the Founder has appeared in the world with the strength *(ki)* of the rising sun; the time has come for the three elements of Heaven, Earth, and Man to come together as one. Thus, our esteemed Kurozumi *Sensei* was born to us on the day, month, and year of the rat,[97] so that he was born with the very heart of Heaven. Then, at the time of the winter solstice of his 35th year, while worshiping the sun, that heart was clearly revealed in his own heart.

Many gathered around him from many places to be blessed with the divine virtue of Amaterasu Ōmikami. The number of his followers grew day after day, month after month, until there were a thousand, or ten thousand — who can reckon the number? Since this Register lists only those well known for their devoted faith, the names here given amount to no more than one percent or one-tenth of a percent of the total number of followers.

> Summer, fourth year of
> Koka (1847)
> Signed with awe and
> sincerity,
> Tokio Katsutarō

Before recounting the activities of the Founder's most important disciples of this period, let us note another important memorial to him. In that same year (1847), on the day of the winter solstice, Matsuda Suigai, a retainer of the Ikusaka clan, painted a portrait of the Founder. Obtaining a dedicatory poem from Kawakami Chūsho, he presented the portrait to Munetada. Kawakami's poem was a formal eulogy in Chinese, consisting of 66 lines of four characters each, praising the virtues of the Founder.

The Direct Disciples II

The early growth of the Way of Amaterasu owed a great deal to the zealous work of a few key people who were directly taught by the Founder, some of whom are known as High Disciples. Two of these, who were among those who joined in ever-increasing numbers between the years 1841 and 1847, are the high disciples Tokio and Akagi.[98] They are included in the list of Four High Disciples that is sometimes referred to.

The name of Tokio Katsutarō was already listed among the followers in 1835, so it was probably about this time that he began to frequent the Founder's home as a follower. He offered his written vow in 1844, about the time he was suffering from osteomyelitis, a disease which affects the bone marrow. In that year the Founder happened to be visiting with Nakayama Tsunejirō, village head of Ogashima in Oku county, in order to give a lecture there. Since this was close to his own home, Tokio thought that he must surely attend a meeting and receive help *(okage)* for his illness. While listening to the Founder speak, Tokio was blessed with a cure for his grave illness and it was at that time that he offered his vow.

Fig. 12   Portrait of Kurozumi Munetada, done in 1847 by
Matsuda Suigai. The calligraphy is a formal eulogy composed
by Kawakami Chūsho. *Courtesy of Kurozumikyō.*

According to the *Record of Tokio's Sermons*, he said:

> Without our great Munetada *Sensei* present in the world, I was just "one patient" *(ikkan)* who would have been finished off by my sickness. Now, I am "a person with a clarified viewpoint" *(ikkan;* i.e., *ichikanja).* With opened eyes I delight to abide in the Way.

It seems that Tokio had been sure he would never get over his illness, but due to Munetada's teachings he was able to receive that blessing *(okage)* and be cured. This brief statement makes vivid and plain his joy at having clear understanding, his eyes opened, living each day with a sense of gratitude. That Nakayama and others from the village offered written vows about the same time is probably a result of Tokio's decision to do so.

From an early age Tokio had loved his studies and was diligent in them. He continued this interest in later life, gathering village children together in a private school *(terakoya)* to teach reading and writing. Being of a sincere and gentle disposition, he was loved and befriended by all the people of the area. Upon becoming a disciple, he sacrificed his family calling entirely, accompanying the Founder on his teaching travels, earnestly listening to the Way, and carrying out his religious practice diligently. Eventually, after the Founder passed away, Tokio came to the forefront of the disciples and was given leadership in missionary activities.

The earnestness of Tokio's religious practice was notable even among the disciples. He had been trained in the Chinese classics, and gained insight into the Way quickly. Though he was not one of the earliest followers, he received the direct guidance of the Founder for seven years, and Munetada gave him a name — Munemichi — that employed one of the Chinese characters used in his own name. This indicates the Founder's recognition of his devotedness to the Way.

One year the Founder instructed him make a visit to Ise Shrine in his stead. After completing his preparations, he went to say goodbye before leaving. The Founder said to him:

> I want you to put your whole heart and soul into the pilgrimage to Ise Shrine you are taking on my behalf at this time. By all means, do not come back until you have held an audience with Amaterasu Ōmikami.

These instructions troubled Tokio all the way to Ise. He could not understand how he could have "an audience with Amaterasu" as he had been told. On reaching an inn in Yamada, near the Shrine, he purified his mind and body before entering to worship at the Inner *(Naiku)* Shrine. He returned to worship many times, and while praying with single-hearted devotion suddenly had the sensation that he really had met with Amaterasu

Ōmikami. He experienced an indescribable feeling of gratitude, and the following poem came to him:

> A little story
>   Told in the distant mountains
>   Of far-off China
>   Is something that can be heard
>   Even without hearing.

He had been blessed with the graces of Heaven. After offering even more prayers, he returned and reported to Munetada what had happened. Tokio was a very sincere and sensitive individual, and the Founder was continually cautioning, "Tokio-san, you must show more pride in yourself." In complete contrast, to Akagi he would constantly give another kind of warning, "There is nothing as terrible as self-conceit. Don't ever forget that." The Founder's teaching was adapted to the individual characteristics of each person (*Tales of the Founder* 47).

It was Tokio who was designated by the Founder to write the introduction for the *Register of Disciples*. To be chosen from among the numerous followers says again how much trust the Founder had in him. As if to live up to that trust, Tokio devoted himself solely to his faith and to the spreading of the Way. Thus, when later on the High Disciples' Grand Missionary Campaign Resolution was made, Tokio took charge of the eastern parts of Bizen and of Harima. Since Harima, today part of Hyōgo Prefecture, was at that time completely virgin territory as far as missionary work was concerned, the difficulties and hardships he suffered there were immense, quite apart from his responsibilities in Bizen.

In his missionary efforts he centered his activities either in Himeji city or in Miki city. Unfortunately, he met with many obstacles in the course of his work, such as the miracles which occurred being mistaken for "Christian black magic."[99] Reportedly there were times when he was put into jail. The following poem of his refers to his activities at this time:

> How could I know
>   It would not be rich brocade
>   I'd wear in honor
>   But the wet robes of slander
>   When I came home again.

But on reconsideration, he sang:

> It does not matter
>   How many slanderous layers
>   Of wet robes I wear
>   Keeping clear this heart of mine
>   Is what will quickly dry me.

Tokio became one of the great teachers in behalf of his revered Munetada. He believed that the Way of Amaterasu Ōmikami was unequaled in all the world, the highest, greatest path of all. This is why he gave everything he had to spreading the word, having no doubt he would be fully successful and return home laden with honors. However, in reality the opposite occurred. He was unjustly misunderstood and the subject of suspicion, which was more than his heart could bear. Yet, if he would keep his own individual heart clear, these groundless suspicions and misunderstandings would certainly melt away and there would come a time of understanding. Furthermore, he told himself repeatedly, he must persevere until that time arrived.

Not of a wealthy family to begin with, Tokio's tendency not to take note of his family calling and finances, coupled with the close attention he paid to preaching the Way, seems to have made difficulties for his wife. It was not just the hurdles due to misunderstandings while carrying on preaching activity in the outside world which had to be overcome, but the many economic problems as well. When setting off to preach, he would take with him clothing and money for travel expenses which his wife would so carefully prepare, but then on his return, he would have left only the clothes on his back.

At the time when the petition requesting the granting of the status of *Daimyōjin* for the Founder was being initiated, Tokio is said to have written this poem:

Since we have been blessed
    By Amaterasu's Way
        And divine virtue,
Those who are above the clouds
    Can also follow the Way.[100]

He was gentle and modest by nature, but on his travels alone to preach the Way, his enthusiastic heart inspired those who heard him speak, and in various places miracles occurred. It is said that his sermons were quite distinctive in character, in accord with his unusual personality.

In the 11th month of 1845, Akagi Tadaharu, later one of the High Disciples, entered the Way. Akagi was by nature a large-hearted man not often bothered by trivial matters, and also very earnest and fond of learning. When just 20 years old, he had become an adopted son of the Akagi family, married into it to become its eventual head. Two years later he lost his eyesight, and though his efforts to find a cure were exhaustive, nothing came of them and he began to sink into despair. In later 1845 a relative by the name of Nishimura Saisuke, who had recently become a follower, suggested that he attend one of Munetada's lectures. Being a considerably well-read person, Akagi's education and temperament would not allow him to believe that listening to a sermon would restore his eyesight, so he was not easily persuaded.

Eventually, just to please his relative who continued to encourage him, he did agree to make an appearance at a meeting. While listening to his very first sermon and without at all intending it, Akagi was drawn into the words he heard, experiencing for the first time the sense of wonder and gratitude of a world he had never known before. He was deeply impressed with the sermon which spoke of being "one with Kami." After eight years of blindness his eyesight was instantly restored and he entered upon the Way. It was at this time that he wrote the following poem:

> Waking from my dream
>   looking at my dwelling place
>   all my heart and mind
> Held securely in the arms
>   of blessed shining Heaven.[101]

Akagi, a man of strong emotions and wholehearted in his convictions, was able after attending just one sermon to open up to an entirely new way of thinking. Quickly he established a firm belief that there was no other way than this Way, and he quickly gained an experiential grasp of the Way as well. This was so even though the time he spent under the direct

Fig. 13   The main gate *(Zuijinmon)* of the Omoto Munetada Shrine. In popular thought, the pillars at the two sides are associated with his two central disciples *(Kokumon)*, Akagi Tadaharu and Tokio Katsutarō. *Courtesy of Kurozumikyō.*

guidance of the Founder was shorter than that of Tokio, only four years in length. Like Tokio, Akagi received a character from Munetada's name to form his religious honorary name, which was Tadaharu. These two are considered to be the two main pillars among the Kurozumi disciples *(Kokumon)* because their achievements in spreading the Way were so outstanding.

When the High Disciples held their Grand Missionary Campaign conference shortly after the death of the Founder, it was initially decided that Bizen, Bitchu, and Mimasaka (Okayama Prefecture), and the surrounding areas of Bingo (Hiroshima Prefecture), Izumo (Shimane Prefecture), Inaba and Hoki (Tottori Prefecture), and Harima (Hyōgo Prefecture), would be targeted for missionary work. It is said, however, that Akagi strongly urged that Yamashiro (Kyoto) should also be included since it was the location of the Imperial Palace at the time. After deliberation about who would be best in which area, it was decided that Akagi who had been the advocate of Yamashiro would be responsible for it, and he set off for Kyoto in high spirits to begin what would become a magnificently successful missionary enterprise.

The first thing that those working in Kyoto realized was that though they viewed Munetada as a savior, he was not recognized as such by the general public. Particularly in a city such as Kyoto, rich in shrines and temples, they soon decided that above all it was necessary for the Founder to be publicly recognized as a kami in order for them to get a hearing. Among his followers, Munetada was already being referred to as *Daimyōjin,* but this was not yet a formal designation and they launched a campaign to have this title officially bestowed on him.[102]

The opinion of the Yoshida family, who were the officials in charge of granting such titles, was that no matter how great a person Munetada may have been, such a short period of time had passed since his death that it was quite impossible to bestow upon him the requested title. Akagi's view, however, was that there had never been anyone like Munetada, so that lack of precedents should not stand in the way. Thus, rather than withdraw the request, he worked with firmer resolve, putting his heart and soul into the task until eventually he presented to the Yoshida family a "Petition for the Title of *Daimyōjin.*" Eventually the Yoshidas were moved by Akagi's enthusiasm and devotion to admit the greatness of the divine Founder in accomplishing many miracles, and in 1856 they granted it.

Akagi's efforts during this time are indeed great amidst difficulties, his active preaching and teaching among the aristocrats being particularly notable. Nobles from the Kujo, Nijo, Rokujo, and other families of the Imperial Court offered their written vows one after another and entered the Way. There is a report that the Emperor Kōmei also was initiated by these nobles. A poem composed by Lord Rokujo Arifusa reads as follows:

If this deity
    Did not give us the blessings
        Of Amaterasu
How then could we have entered
    The Way of Sincerity.

A bit later than the others, Prince Sanjo Sanetomi and his wife also became followers.

Akagi's efforts were not directed only toward the upper class. He also put forth continuing strong efforts among commoners. When the Munetada Shrine, built at Kaguraoka in a corner of Yoshida Hill in the northeast quarter of Kyoto, was completed in the second month of 1862, worshipers from far and near flooded the shrine. The following poem by Akagi celebrates the completion of the Munetada Shrine:

The foundation is laid
    Here at Kaguraoka
        On Yoshida hill
Now across the capital
    A divine breeze will blow.

Fig. 14   The Munetada Shrine at Kaguraoka, on the grounds of the Yoshida Shrine in the northeast section of Kyoto. Munetada Kami was enshrined here in 1862 with the official kami rank of *Daimyōjin. Courtesy of Kurozumikyō.*

Throughout the time that he was promoting the faith in the Kyoto area, Akagi followed a policy expressed in this brief epigram:

Receiving only the blessing of *Daimyōjin* upon my head, and wishing sincerely to save all people under Heaven from suffering.

— from *Akagi's Evening Talks*

His poetry shows us his complete and constant confidence in the Divine Founder:

Looking up I see
   Growing even higher
   A deified teacher
And basking in his blessings
   I take pleasure in their joy.

Though my virtue is small
   I'm now called Tadaharu
   After Munetada
And I go throughout the land
   By the grace [*on*] of that Kami.[103]

Deified Teacher
   Now that you have been enshrined
   This heart of mine
Never for a moment wants
   To ever leave your side.

The Six High Disciples

Together with the four disciples Ishio, Kawakami, Tokio, and Akagi, an additional two — Hoshijima Ryōhei and Morishita Keitan — make up a group referred to as the Six High Disciples.

Hoshijima Ryōhei lost his father while still very young and was raised single-handedly by his mother. She often asked Munetada for advice and guidance in bringing up her son, regarding him as a kind of substitute father for him. Since the Founder provided that for the still very young Ryōhei, they would often frequent his home. In 1843, while still a boy of 14, Ryōhei made a written pledge and joined the following.

For generations the Hoshijima family had been in the service of the Amaki clan, located in present-day Kurashiki near Okayama, as scholars of the Chinese classics. At an early age, however, Ryōhei hated to read books. On returning home after lessons with his teacher, he would toss his bundle of books into the house from the entrance way and run off to play. The mother, at a loss for what to do about it, consulted with Munetada, who advised, "Rather than force him to read, which he doesn't like to do, convince him slowly to like books."

Thereafter she would suppress the part of herself that wanted to force him to read and instead say such things as, "I see you're going to take your books and go to your room, but are you really going to read them? That would really please me," and reward him with sweets, until Ryōhei, though just a child, began to feel a sense of obligation to his mother and began reading his books. Day by day he was praised for reading and encouraged to read more, until in due course he came to find reading interesting and eventually became quite scholarly (*Tales of the Founder* suppl. 4).

No one, no matter who it is, will react negatively to praise. Cultivating someone's ability by praising his or her good points is what the Founder often referred to in his teachings as "making the best of things" *(ikasu)*. In this way the hidden potential in people may be brought out.[104] It is a way of putting vibrancy into one's inner heart, and it is essential to training in religious practice.

Once when Ryōhei was paying a visit to the Founder, Munetada asked him to give a lecture on the Analects of Confucius. When Ryōhei took out the text and began reading, the Founder sat down in a lower seat and listened earnestly, keeping his head bowed and both hands on the floor in full respect. Ryōhei was rather surprised by this, and asked, "Why are you listening so intently to a sermon by someone like me?" To this Munetada replied, "Well, what you are reading now are the teachings of a sage. That is why I am listening so respectfully. This is how one must always listen to the teachings of a holy man." In this way the Founder gave him a vivid example of the right attitude to learning from sages. Ryōhei's intellectual appetite was aroused all the more as a result.

The Founder reportedly once said to Hoshijima,

> The Way of Amaterasu Ōmikami will meet with increasingly good fortune from now on. There will undoubtedly be people who will record the teachings of the Way so as to pass them on to others, and you may be among them.

After the Meiji Restoration, Ryōhei did devote himself to writing down the teachings of the Founder. Later he became the head of the Educational Division at Kurozumikyō headquarters. Starting with the *Short Biography of our Founder Munetada* and *The Teaching of the Sincere Heart*, and on to *The Thirty Guidelines of the Way*, and *The Hundred and Twenty Sayings of the Founder*,[105] he edited the teachings of the Founder so that they could be more easily understood. He had a far-reaching effect in setting the direction educational activity should go.

Morishita Tatsutarō, known by his religious name of Keitan, entered the following in 1844. Though a samurai of the Bizen clan, he received an extremely small stipend, and ever since childhood had been subject to financial hardship. However, Morishita had twice the fighting spirit of most and when he set his mind to something, he would carry it out to the end.

Here is how Morishita became a follower. He heard that a faith healer had appeared in Nakano village. Thinking that this was misleading to the public, he felt he should do something to expose the imposter. So, he set off for Nakano, willing if necessary even to kill the fraudulent person. Morishita's arrival in the village corresponded to a meeting day, and as usual, Munetada was giving a sermon. Seating himself in the back row, he listened to the sermon and was moved by what he heard. After Munetada finished speaking, Morishita questioned him further, and though it was quite contrary to his original intent, he was thoroughly charmed and drawn to the path of which the Founder spoke. Reportedly, he offered a written pledge on the spot and became a disciple.

Thereafter, as an influential member of the Banchō monthly meeting,[106] he worked diligently for his faith. Later, just prior to the Meiji Restoration, he organized a troop of soldiers from the farming class and fought in a number of encounters in various places across the country. His service was quite meritorious, and in 1872 he was appointed the governor (*Kenrei*) of Oita Prefecture. In that office he earnestly propagated the faith of Kurozumikyō.

In 1876, when Kurozumikyō was granted permission by the Meiji government to become an independent sect of Shinto, Morishita was called upon to serve as Vice Patriarch of Kurozumikyō.

In that office he was responsible for many internal and external matters, assisting the Third Patriarch, Muneatsu,[107] in such varied activities as negotiations with government offices, religious instruction inside the organization, spreading the faith to others, and other aspects as well. His accomplishments are many and he is remembered with much respect.

Another side of Morishita's character should also be told. When the subject of building a shrine for Munetada (completed in 1885) first was discussed, there were two opposing groups on the question of where it should be built. One advocated Munetada's birthplace (Omoto) as the site, and the other proposed the hilly region to the east of Okayama. At the time, Morishita strongly supported the latter, but when discussion ended and the Patriarch (Muneatsu) had ruled in favor of Omoto, Morishita firmly supported that decision. Despite the fact that it was contrary to his original preference, he was the first to donate money. He donated 7700 yen, equivalent to several tens of millions in today's purchasing power, to the building fund. Morishita was a man of simple means and not blessed with much inheritance or property. He had raised this money by saving the honorarium fees he had received when out preaching in various parts of the country.

Discussing what needed to be discussed, but abiding by and giving one's all to a decision once made, is the true essence of modern democracy. It also was a characteristic of Morishita.

Towards the end of his life (he died in 1890), Morishita often said to people:

> In all my activities in this world, whether it be military matters, political affairs or whatever, by following the teachings of Kurozumikyō devotedly I never departed from what is proper and I stayed free of mistakes.

In addition to Morishita, other men of real talent, such as Omori Busuke, Ishida Rokuzaemon, Okamoto Kyōzaemon, Takeuchi Raizō, Kobayashi Kenzō, Komoto Taisuke, Ikeda Chiyozō, Nonoue Tatewaki, and others, joined the following as clouds gathering in the sky, one after another.

Fig. 15   The Munetada Shrine in the Omoto section of Okayama. Munetada Kami was enshrined here in 1885. This and the Kaguraoka shrine were the two principal shrines of Kurozumiky until the *Daikyōden* at Shintozan was completed in 1974. *Courtesy of Kurozumikyō.*

Building the Kurozumi House

The proposal for construction of a new residence for Munetada had been put forth in the 11th month of 1846, with the Founder securing a construction permit at that time. About a year and half later, in the fourth month of 1848, the house was finished and a completion ceremony was held not long after. The "Record of Gifts Received" written at that time lists 80 people who gave congratulatory gifts.

Among them should be noted Kōzaki Kodenji, Deyashiki Kokichi, and Sakurai Kimata, who offered congratulatory calligraphy saying, respectively, "Donating all gloom," "Having no doubts," and "Free of all impurity." It was a joyful time, full of wit and humor. The record also contains a list of gifts to the paid craftsmen and other workers, expressing thanks to them, as well as an entry which states that approximately 245 beggars were given alms of 2 pieces of silver each.

The contents of the calligraphy might seem a bit peculiar as congratulatory gifts, but what the three individuals meant in referring to "gloom," "doubt," and "impurity" was that they were dedicating themselves to live from that day forward with joy *(yōki)* in their hearts, and asking for the help of the Founder in maintaining that joyous state. They had a sincere and humble attitude, having in mind the "true building of the Founder's house."

The Founder lived about a year and ten months in the new house. It is today for the most part in the same condition in which it was at that time. The altar at which he prayed morning and night, the platform and room where he gave his sermons, and the four-and-a-half *tatami* mat room which served as both his studying room and living quarters, all still exist. Followers and others often visit the house and are struck by how vividly they can imagine the days of the Founder, helping them renew their reverence for him.

In the sixth month of 1848 Munetada's first grandchild, Gonkichi, later known as Muneatsu (1848-1880), was born. This happened at a time when, as already mentioned, the number of followers was increasing daily, the Way was flourishing, and Munetada's home and new central lecture hall was being completed. Munetada's long-held and heartfelt desire for the opening of good fortune *(kaiun)* of the Way of Amaterasu Ōmikami was now realized. It was in the midst of all this that Muneatsu was born, and the followers, not to mention Munetada himself, undoubtedly saw him as part of that fulfillment.

In later life Muneatsu played an important role in establishing the Kurozumikyō organization. He was third in line from the Founder, losing his father in 1856 while still young. After that he spent some time in Kyoto, even staying for a while with the Kujo family, chief advisors *(Kampaku)* to the emperor. After the Meiji restoration he spent some years in Tokyo, the new capital, active in the petition movement seeking approval of Kurozumikyō as an independent religious body under the government policy of the times.

He then became the first head *(Kanchō)* of Kurozumikyō after the government's recognition was given. The foundation of the present-day Kurozumikyō organization, as well as the enshrinement of Munetada in the Main Shrine building at Omoto, are products of Muneatsu's time. In all this Muneatsu was a central figure as the third in line.

Iku's Passing Away

The great happiness of 1848 did not, however, last very long. In the same year as Muneatsu's birth, on the eighth day of the 10th month, Munetada's wife Iku passed away to Heaven. For more than 40 years, since 1806, she had accompanied him and served him. In the background of his splendid career we may see the humble support and sincere modesty, the wifely loyalty and love, she showed Munetada.

When at age 33 he lay at home in his sick bed, sunk deep in sorrow at the sudden loss of his parents, she nursed him with loving care. This may not seem like such an unusual thing, but it certainly made a large contribution to his gaining the completely new viewpoint that resulted from his enlightenment, and the new belief in Amaterasu Ōmikami in which he became established. When he was away on preaching trips and worshipers would come to their house, she would extend warm and courteous hospitality to them.

When he was lecturing nearby or even at a distance, she would often finish her household chores quickly and join the other worshipers who had gathered in the lecture hall. On these occasions, it is said that Munetada would stop in the middle of his sermon and say:

> Ah, Iku, you have come. Listen, everyone, my wife, after taking care of the house and the children, has come tonight. She is showing such devotion. It really must be admired.
>
> *Tales of the Founder* 65

The story is also told that often, if Iku would take a little too long to come out of the washroom, Munetada would move closer and ask, "Iku, are you all right?" (*Tales of the Founder* 28).

They were truly a happily married couple with great affection for each other, and they were looked upon and respected by the followers as a model couple. However, on the eighth day of the 10th month, nearing the end of fall and the advent of winter, Iku regrettably passed away at the age of 64.

How great the Founder's sorrow must have been. Munetada, spiritually enlightened to why things happen as they do in the universe, was usually so absorbed in his religious work that nothing could distract him. The shock of Iku's death, however, so greatly moved him that he became lost in sorrow.

The story is told that he was sitting formally beside her when she took her last breath. He had fallen asleep just then. Soon afterward he muttered quietly to himself, "Ah, I have done something foolish *(gebi).*" By that he seems to have meant something like "I have done something awkward," or "I have done something shameful."

The poems *(uta)* the Founder wrote at the time of his loss are:

> The world of dreams
> > Is, I know, a world of dreams,
> > > Yet I cannot waken. . .
> For another yet to wake
> > I know I shall be longing.
> > > > > *O-uta* 193

> Although I have heard
> > That the flowers of yesterday
> > > Are dreams of today,
> Towards this storm that rages
> > I hold a deep resentment.
> > > > > *O-uta* 194

Then, after thinking things over:

> Flowers of the world
> > Scattered everywhere about...
> > > let it then be so.
> I will bring the boundless Way
> > to bloom again everywhere.
> > > > > *O-uta* 195

Almost all the Founder's numerous *uta* talk of gratitude and joy, and, other than the first two above, there are none which could be called bitter. These exceptions show the extent of his grief at his wife's death.

Then we see, however, in the *uta* written after thinking things over, that Munetada was not one to remain flooded by sorrow. His loss led him to remember the mission entrusted to him by Amaterasu Ōmikami, to work toward the everlasting blooming of the Way everywhere under Heaven and on Earth. His mind thus was renewed in commitment to the Great Way's prospering.

When, as was related in Chapter 5, the husband of his daughter passed away, the Founder lamented that one can never be sure of what is going to happen next, but added that everything that happens is a chance to gain fresh insight. The true meaning of the Great Way is religious practice at every moment. Another story showing another aspect of this point concerns a follower who had recently lost a parent, yet did not allow himself to grieve in the least, believing that was how someone should act who was practicing the Way. The Founder said to him, "You are seriously mistaken. Seeing a parent die is part of the practice of the Way."

He knew that people need feelings of pity and sympathy. Compassion and affection between parent and child, husband and wife, friend and friend are the most beautiful, precious things we enjoy in our lives. Without feelings, people become merely parched mummies. Sorrow at the death of a loved one is an expression of these emotions, and it is natural for anyone to feel them.

On the other hand, he always advised his followers to "develop your sense of pity and sympathy, but don't be led astray in feeling them." It was when his wife died that he truly showed in his own bodily life the meaning of this advice. His followers can look to his example.

His Final Sermon

In 1849 Munetada turned 70 years old, and the end of his physical life was approaching. In the sixth month of that year his third daughter, Tome, passed away. Soon after, in the eighth month, his long-time live-in disciple and assistant, Ginjibei, also passed on. These two deaths in rapid succession may have been too much for Munetada, and in the 11th month he delivered his final sermon, never to rise to the teaching platform again. However, it was not for this kind of reason that he decided to step down.

Some time earlier, he had said to Munenobu's wife, Kaji, one day as she was combing his hair, "Be prepared for the time when I can no longer give sermons." Also, about the middle of the eleventh month, it is said he told his granddaughter as she was removing her coat after returning from an outing, "The time will come when I will shed my body just as you take off your coat."

From this and other things the Founder said around this time, it appears the idea of moving to another stage was on his mind. As the Way kept spreading Munetada received more and more invitations from people. There being only one of him, he felt that he couldn't possibly attend to all that was expected. Thus, as is believed, the Founder's heartfelt wish was to separate from his body, freeing himself so that he could be in various places at once, enabling him to save anyone as needed. This was the deeper reason why he stopped giving sermons.

His Ascension to Heaven

From the 11th month of 1849 Munetada gradually became weaker. His little grandson, Gonkichi, stayed with him as his companion, and until the second month of 1850 Munetada spent his days in relative ease. His weakness increased, however, until eventually he was confined to his bed.

About the 22nd or 23rd of the month, the principal disciples, including Kawakami Chūsho and Ishio Kensuke, came one after the other to pay him sick calls. When Kawakami visited, the two talked of many things until Kawakami finally asked, "How are you feeling?" to which the Founder replied, "I feel like that poem that Okamoto Rin wrote." At the end of the previous year, Okamoto Mankichi's daughter, Rin, and his son had together composed a poem which read:

> If we live our lives
>   By entrusting everything
>   To the Deity,
> Then we will feel very good
>   At the closing of the year.

Mankichi, thinking the poem quite good, had brought it to show Munetada, who also praised it highly but wanted to change the last line of it, making it read "at the closing of the day." By doing so he was saying that we should feel this way not just once a year, but live with this feeling every day.

It seems that he said this kind of thing often in his sermons, and it was well known among the followers of that time. As he neared the end of his life, he still felt gratitude in his heart for every minute of every day.

Around the same time, Omori Busuke's son, also named Busuke, paid a visit to Munetada in his sickbed. The Founder had not eaten for a number of days and was looking very haggard and worn. Busuke had lost his own father not long before (in the tenth month of 1848), and his eyes welled up with tears as he looked upon the haggard figure of Munetada, whom he had long revered and admired. Noticing this, the Founder asked him:

> What are you worrying about? Physical illnesses are nothing but clouds that veil the earth. When the wind blows, the sky clears, so don't worry. Continue on with your religious studies.

At the time Busuke was only 20 years old.

As Munetada was in such poor condition, he was permitted very few visitors, though he was looked up to by so many as a living kami who had rescued many from their suffering. Finally, at daybreak on the 25th day of the second month of 1850, Munetada went to his rest.

The Founder had previously said:

There is but one path
Through all of Heaven and Earth
The Way I have taught
It brings us all-surpassing joy
To continue to walk in this path.[108]

With joy in his heart, he had earnestly followed the Way and shown others the path as well, before ascending to rest in the High Plains of Heaven.[109]

The Effects of the Founder's Life

In reviewing Munetada's life, we see that he did indeed achieve the goals he had set for himself as a young dutiful son, of becoming a living Kami and thus establishing the names of his parents in the next world. When he was 33 years old, the sorrow at the loss of his parents forced him to his sickbed. When his sickness had taken a turn for the worse and he was near death, he was revived through divine grace and then gained his great spiritual wisdom. Graciously accepting the Divine Mission given him, the Founder actively promulgated the Way of Amaterasu Ōmikami for a period of 37 years.

Just how many sick and troubled people he rescued is not countable, though during his lifetime there were thousands of followers, possibly as many as 200,000, among whom were many great disciples. Then, his son Munenobu succeeded to his position when he turned 29, becoming the second Patriarch. From that time forward Munetada had been free to pursue his mission of saving people and aiding everyone with increasing effect, making known the blessings of Amaterasu Ōmikami for all the people of the world.

On the day of the funeral, some of the disciples found it difficult to hide their sorrow at the passing of their great Teacher. They wondered what obstacles would arise in the spreading of the Way without him, and some voiced their pessimism. Kimura Seiemon spoke up at that time and said to the others,

Once I was told this by our great teacher. When I asked him, "Is your spirit and body immortal?" he replied, "To save many people at once I will shed my body and my spirit and will fly freely in any direction." The future of the Way is before us. From now on it will blossom. I'm certain it will blossom.

This speech reflected not only Kimura's sentiments, but probably those of most of the disciples who felt that the precious path that had been opened for them by the Founder could not just be left as it was then. The Founder had given up his role out of a desire that the divine blessings be spread even further. As his disciples, they felt they should comply with his heart and work together to lay a course for the spreading of the Way.

When the funeral services were over, the disciples decided to meet again at the fifty-day service. During their second meeting, on the 15th day of the fourth month, the duties of each individual in the High Disciples' Grand Missionary Campaign were decided, with someone being assigned to each area targeted for missionary work. The plan was made to begin that summer with the epoch-making missionary campaign. They were intent on carrying the campaign forward no matter what would happen.

During his lifetime, the Founder's activity had been limited almost entirely to the bounds of present-day Okayama Prefecture, except for the six times he went to the Ise Shrine. With this broad promulgation campaign his teachings began gradually to gain a foothold in areas outside the prefecture. Notably, the petition campaign in Kyoto for the title of *Daimyōjin* and the construction of Munetada Shrine at Kaguraoka were remarkable steps forward. With the coming of the Meiji Period, Muneatsu worked extraordinarily hard to obtain approval for the Kurozumi *Kyōdan* in accordance with the policies of the new government. In 1872 the organization was recognized, and in 1876 permission was granted to form Kurozumi Shinto as a separate and independent sect. This was the foundation for today's Kurozumikyō.

When we recall the trials which the disciples endured during that time, we realize how much they wished to save other people in the world by showing them, even one by one, the Way which had saved their own lives and brought them so much joy. This was also the one great desire of the Founder.

So, since they were carrying out his wish, the disciples firmly believed that the Founder would help and guide them.

Do not look for me
    In my present form any more
        You will not find it;
Simply, in Earth and Heaven,
    Something shining everywhere.[110]

The blessings of the Founder dwell in this world, and he is always nearby to guide and assist us along the Way.

I, Sakyo, will lead you to Amaterasu Ōmikami's side. May you all follow me.

Those who follow the teacher Sakyo will certainly not be left to suffer alone.

These words were repeatedly spoken during the regular lectures. To follow the master meant nothing less than to submit oneself to his guidance. The most important thing for the followers of the Way to do is to "obey that guidance." By living accordingly, one receives the blessings of Amaterasu Ōmikami, thus leading a bright and joyful life.

In turn, one must work for the sake of others and the world, helping to spread these precious guiding principles to the peoples of the world so that they, too, may share in the blessings of Amaterasu and be happy.

This is the sacred desire of Amaterasu Ōmikami, the guardian of this universe, as it is also the great wish of the Founder Munetada. This desire has been handed on to us by these numerous early members, and it is the spirit of all Kurozumi disciples today.

Fig. 16   A group of members praying at *Nippai* at the top of the hill at Shintozan. The sun is not itself the object of prayer, but only presents the spiritual presence of Amaterasu Ōmikami, with whom Munetada Kami is united ("not-two"). *Courtesy of Kurozumikyō.*

Appendix

Stories of the Founder[111]

I

Apologizing for Disturbing His Heart

Once, while he was on his way to see Mr. Mori, village head at Kmoto-mura, *Kyōso*[112] was crossing a one-plank bridge over the Sunagawa stream. This was just after a heavy rain and the bridge was almost flooded over by the rushing water. When he was halfway across, the plank shifted with a sudden wobble. Without his intending it, the inner heart *(bunshin)* within *Kyōso* was ruffled by the sudden jolt.

After he had crossed over and gotten up on the bank, he sat down in formal fashion on the grass, wearing his *hakama*. He offered a formal apology to Amaterasu Ōmikami for the way he had lost his inner calm. Though it might seem a small thing, he thought he had behaved badly.

It is quite natural that a plank bridge would be unsteady in the midst of a flood of water like that, and that a person crossing over might be startled, even for just an instant. Even so, *Kyōso* offered an apology for allowing his heart to be disturbed.

If that is what he did, what should those whose hearts have been disturbed and dismayed with sufferings over a long period do? What sort of apology should they offer? When we ponder on this experience of *Kyōso*, we are led to revere him with awe.

II

Reverencing His Wife and Offering Prayer to Her

Whenever *Kyōso* returned home from some mission, Madame Iku always met him at the door and greeted him politely with a cup of tea and with cordial words of thanks,

Oh, thank you for the trouble you have gone to. You must be tired.

In response, *Kyōso* used to clap his hands. After holding his hands together in prayer for a moment he would accept the cup with reverence and drink the tea with thanks.
One of his disciples who had observed this so often once asked him,

Why is it that you drink the tea your wife has prepared for you with such reverence? And especially, why do this just the way we offer prayers to Kami?

He replied,

The reason is what I always say when I preach, that in every person's heart there dwells the divine presence, so graciously and kindly. That is my reason for doing it.
    Remember also that when we stop being so busy with our own heart's concerns we become one with Kami who is within us, and eventually we will, in all humility, be one of the eight million kami.[113]
    My wife does not originally belong to me. In her origin she is just another "divine child of Kami." And, when we do depart from our own self and leave behind all self-concerned and evil thoughts, we return instantly to the original divine state.
    Well, when I come home from outside, Iku simply tries to give me comfort, serving me a cup of tea with a sincere and whole heart. There is not a speck of evil in her. So pure and innocent! At that moment I see Kami within her. She is, in fact, Kami to me. That is the reason I reverence her, and enjoy my tea with feelings of respect and gratitude toward her.

On this point, some people use the expression "respect for the dignity of humanity." *Kyōso's* posture is much more advanced. His attitude is one of "respect to the divine dignity." This is what he has taught us. If we could only advance to the level where we could respect others' divinity, all conflicts, differences, and disagreements could be solved and all quarrels would disappear.

III

Feelings of Friendship among Followers at Meetings[114]

One follower related the following story, years after this happened:

1

The meetings on the "two and seven" days were well attended. We rarely failed to go, but there were others who came from even greater distances and who had to return home again that same night. I don't know how it is now, but in those days there was a sword rack at the entrance and a number of swords were placed there. It looked very impressive, but we took off our straw raincoats and put them down next to the rack anyway before entering the house.

The place was filled with worshipers, including some from leading samurai families in service to the Ikeda clan, such as the Furutas and the Ishidas. There was no segregation, however, in which one person was given a seat of honor because he was a samurai, or another had to sit in a less desirable seat because he was a farmer. No matter who it was, even a merchant or an artisan, whoever arrived first got the front seats. All were seated in the order that they arrived.

2

On this particular day it seemed that some important people had to sit in inconvenient places at the back, with low-born people bowing to them as they arrived. Some low-born women and children were sitting up front in the better seats. The samurai had much authority at that time and were generally keen on their dignity, but at these meetings they often could not get seats near where *Kyōso* was preaching, or sometimes even get a place inside where they could see well. In those days you would not see that happening anywhere else.

Once the meeting began there was absolute silence. Once in a while you could hear the clap of hands *(kashiwade)* but that was all. No noise came from anyone, even the women and children. But this was not caused by any kind of rigid formality. The voice of the Founder sank into us, deep into our hearts. We were so deeply moved that our heads became heavy and we felt nothing but gratitude and the sanctity of the moment.

Once the meeting was over, we could not remember anything that had been said, though I have an excellent memory about everything else. Even now at about the age of sixty I can remember the time at which small things happened long ago. I am sometimes called a "living diary." But I can't remember anything *Kyōso* preached at one of those meetings. Of course, I came to understand that it is not necessary to remember what was said. That was not the point. It was important simply to be filled with gratitude.

After the sermon there was *majinai* for those who had asked for it, again on a first-come-first-served basis. Those who needed healing were lying down on the *tatami* mats with their heads on pillows, ready to be helped. Once when I was receiving help this way, Kurozumi Sensei said, as he pressed my abdomen firmly,

"Oh, by the way, I do hope Kamezo is enjoying good health these days. I have received letters of invitation from him. But, I am sorry that various engagements and activities have kept me so busy that, to my regret, I have been unable to accept his invitation. Would you please convey the message to him, with my sincere apology, that I will arrange my schedule to fulfill his wishes."

Up to this day I can recall the message he entrusted to me, down to its minute points.

3

After everyone who had asked for *majinai* had received it, we all took part in a dinner together, and then the meeting was considered to be over. This was usually around ten at night.

Afterwards everyone mingled together freely. *Kyōso* treated everyone equally in a free and friendly fashion, with the sick getting special and careful attention. As a result, whenever the followers happened to meet somewhere it was like meeting members of a family. We enjoyed a feeling of mutual closeness and care for each other.

On one occasion as I was hurrying home from a meeting I happened to catch up to some samurai, five or six of them. They were walking ahead of me on the path and also going home from the same meeting. In those days someone of my social rank was not allowed to pass samurai on the road. I was going along behind them for a while when they turned and asked me very politely how far I had to go. When I answered that I was going to Shimoyamada in Oku county they apologized for holding me up when I had so far to go.

Well, well. That's a long way. Don't worry about us. Please go on ahead, and be careful on your way home.

This was, I knew, because of the Way, and I felt deeply grateful.

This unadorned story of the old days says in clear and simple words what kind of atmosphere was fostered among the followers at that time, how friendly and cordial the relationship among us was. It sparkles like a pure jewel, full of the companionship enjoyed by the different members. It warms our hearts with satisfaction and gratitude.

IV

At the Doll Shop[115]

One of *Kyōso's* sermons went as follows:

Here is something that happened at a doll shop. An apprentice working there had an accident while dusting the doll displays, the kind used during the girls' festival that have various levels.[116] He was so busily dusting one of them, each of its levels full of dolls, that he hit it so hard with his duster that the whole display fell over.

Now this started some big trouble. All the dolls had fallen off the shelves where they had been so carefully arranged. The apprentice was nervous and confused, and put them back quickly, whichever his hands touched first, without paying attention to where they belonged.

(You see, each of the dolls used in the festival has its own special place on the shelf according to the social status of the people they represent.)

Now see what the apprentice had done. The prince and princess were placed on lower seats, and the guardian samurai were at the top. They were sitting in positions they were not supposed to take, all mixed up.

When the proprietor of the shop saw this he shouted fiercely at the apprentice: "See what you have done! The dolls are all mixed up! Put them back right away where they belong!"

A customer came into the shop just at that time. After quietly watching what was happening, he said to the two of them.

Well, well. What looks like confusion may after all be the right and proper situation. It won't be long before such a time will surely come. I believe the way you have them now must be the right way.

This is the comment he made.

In those days the social status of samurai, farmers, craftsmen, and merchants, in that descending order, was strictly enforced. And it was *Kyōso* who taught every day that everyone is equal. The divided portion *(bunshin)* of the divine presence is equally within everyone, and the eyes of the Great Kami see them so.

He taught the equality of human rights every day in his preaching, often using this story.

— retold by Kurozumi Tadaaki

V

Performing *Majinai* on a Leprosy Patient

1

This is a well-known anecdote that Madame Teruko, *Kyōso's* second daughter, is said to have repeated.

One day a person suffering from leprosy happened to arrive in the city of Okayama after years of wandering from his faraway home. He had been on a miserable and sad journey with no particular destination in mind. He had to beg for his food. He was in terrible shape, with his face half gone and his physical condition gradually deteriorating to the worst, to such a point he could hardly stand it any more.

Still, there were some sympathizers who showed pity on him, and gave him a kind suggestion,

> Why don't you go about one *ri* (four kilometers) west from here, where there is a village called Kaminakano. A living god *(ikigami)* lives there, named Kurozumi. They say those who visit him and receive his blessing of healing prayer are sure to be cured of their illness and relieved of their pain. Why not go see him?

He only half listened to this, and with doubt. No, with 70 per cent doubt and 30 per cent hope. More exactly, with only a few per cent of hope. He was in a desperate situation. He had tried many things, all of which were supposed to be good for him. Nothing had worked out. Still, he was somewhat moved by the kindness and there was nowhere else for him to go. He decided to try this place called Kaminakano. Walking slowly, dragging his handicapped legs, he finally arrived at the gate of *Kyōso's* residence.

2

To his good fortune, *Kyōso* was at home. The poor fellow asked him for a blessing of healing prayer. Sadly looking down at him from his window and seeing his miserable, painful condition, *Kyōso* was unable to conceal or contain his compassion. He invited the man,

> Oh, please do come up into this room. I will be glad to perform *majinai* on you.

He beckoned him into the main room of his residence, the special room where the Great Kami was enshrined and worshiped.

Most likely the poor fellow had been forced to leave his own home, rejected by his relatives and friends as well as his own family, a victim of the dreadful disease of leprosy. Now he was meeting a plump, well-fleshed, kind-looking person with a respectful personality. No doubt it was a great surprise and unexpected happiness that much impressed him as he was shown into the splendid main room.

After offering some purification prayers, *Kyōso* performed his *majinai* conscientiously.

The season was midsummer. *Kyōso,* who weighed well over 200 pounds, blessed the patient so devotedly and wholeheartedly that he was sweating all over his body. Sweat was dripping down all over his face. The same hands he had placed on the half-gone face of the man were now on his own face to wipe off the sweat.

At that moment Madame Iku entered the room, returning from some errand outside. When she saw *Kyōso's* face she gave a terrible, involuntary cry of surprise.

She shouldn't be blamed for that. It was quite natural. *Kyōso's* hands and face were covered with the man's ugly, bloody pus.

3

As for the patient, it was the first time since he had been infected with his horrible disease, or perhaps it was the first time in his whole life, that he had experienced such a deep impression of sympathy. He forgot his physical and mental pain, worry, and despair. When he saw what he owed to Kami through the guidance of *Kyōso,* he began to think of the divine virtue and blessings of Kami. And, when he was offered a corner of an outbuilding to sleep in, he was again touched with gratitude.

When the man had gone out of the main room, Madame Iku recovered her composure and said,

It was good to perform *majinai.* But please remember that in this room we enshrine the Great Kami. We must keep it clean. I don't believe it is good to stain and soil this room. I don't worry about you giving healing prayers for people, but when I saw you had gotten yourself so dirty, I was just overcome by surprise.

Hearing her words, *Kyōso* responded gently,

You may be right, but... When I saw the appearance of that poor fellow who came here with the express purpose of seeing me, putting his whole hope and confidence on me and wholly relying on my help, I was overtaken by pity and sympathy. He looked so miserable and hopeless. That is why I could not resist welcoming him into this room. Who could be more miserable than that fellow? He is a person who exactly fits that word.

When that thought came to me, I realized I had to perform *majinai* on him so he would be blessed with the divine virtue of the Great Kami. With my whole mind full of this, I forgot everything and didn't think about the bloody pus getting on my hands. I didn't even realize my hands were covered with it. Since sweat was running all over my face, I used them to wipe myself without thinking about it. I had no idea my face was getting so dirty.

Well, whatever happens now, if we are to fear diseases and feel that such things are dirty and polluting, how could we pray for those who are suffering? Now, let's watch him carefully. Surely he will be blessed with divine virtue.

As expected, before long the fellow was blessed with wonderful divine virtue and was able to enjoy a complete restoration to health.

VI

Introducing Shuzo of Burakuji-mura to the Great Kami

1

Once *Kyōso* was returning home on foot after going on pilgrimage for prayer at the Kiyama Jinja in the province of Mimasaka (north of Okayama city), when he overheard some men behind him talking. They were leading along some horses they were offering for hire, holding their reins as they walked.

> That fellow Shuzo of Burakuji village is so very sick, he is miserably poor, and he lives by himself. And his illness is really very serious. He is so much to be pitied for his pain and suffering.

When these words reached his ears, *Kyōso* realized immediately they were words Heaven wished him to hear. He immediately decided to visit this poor old Shuzo and offer his help. He asked here and there the way to Burakuji-mura. He found out he would need to cover a distance of eight kilometers from where he was, following a path that twisted back and forth over hills and mountains. It was a place about 30 kilometers northeast of Okayama.

"By all means, I must help him to be blessed with divine virtue." With this firm determination, he changed his course and set off to pay Shuzo a visit.

Kyōso found the man's poverty even more pitiful than he had expected. He was living in a tumbledown hut, unsightly to look at, and he was tormented by illness and pain. After a few words of greeting *Kyōso* suggested, "Come on, you can receive the blessing of Kami. I will perform *majinai* on you."

Then he offered his prayers most earnestly. But the man himself was only blaming Heaven for the illness and pain, and cursing the deities. He had not the smallest thought of any kind of faith. Because this was his attitude, there was no room for any miraculous virtue to show up.

Still, *Kyōso* performed his prayers attentively. After telling the man, "Shuzo, please remember that I will continue praying for you, so please wait for the day that you will receive blessings," he left the house.

2

When he had walked for two or three kilometers, he was caught in a sudden shower of rain. It made him think, "That poor Shuzo's roof is broken and there are many holes in it. The rain must be leaking in and harming him."

With this thought he turned around and hurried back. "Shuzo, the roof leaking all over you must be a real problem. I have come back because I am afraid you are in bad trouble."

The man was huddled in one corner of his room, shivering and shaking with cold. *Kyōso* picked up a broom he found there, and praying with all his heart he threw it up to a place where the roof was broken near the sick man and the rain was pouring in. Miraculously, the broom stuck in the hole, stopping it up and preventing any more leaking.

Seeing what was happening, Shuzo was much surprised. He was touched with a strange flash of inspiration. At this moment *Kyōso* blew on him a strong breath of joy *(yōki)*, so as to perform another *majinai* on him.

Shuzo was impressed for the first time in his life with the sincere kindness and courtesy of another person. Struck and overwhelmed by the mysterious power he had witnessed with his own eyes, he was relieved of the illness he had suffered for many years. The divine virtues blessed him with complete recovery.

VII

Put Yourself in the Position of the Seller When You Are Buying Something

1

Madame Iku was not at home one day when the fish peddler came to sell his goods, so *Kyōso* went out in the garden in her place. The peddler had some small fish called *ina* and *tsunashi* which he offered at their average prices, quite reasonable. *Kyōso* nodded his agreement with the price, and bought some ten or twenty fish.

2

When the peddler had left, one of his disciples who was quietly watching all this came over with a grin.

Listen, *Sensei*, I was watching you buy those fish at the price he was asking. You bought them without any dickering about the price.

But that's not what I'm concerned about. You were checking the fish and choosing them very carefully, and I thought you would pick out only the big ones. But instead, you only took the small ones. Excuse my being forward, but I have to admit I think what you were doing was quite peculiar.

This is what I mean: when prices are given at the average, everyone picks the biggest ones and those that look good. The seller knows this, and he knows the larger ones will go first and the smaller ones will be left unsold. Accordingly, he will sooner or later only have the small fish left. Then he will gradually lower the prices to sell them off. So, at the beginning he raises his prices.

These are things everybody knows, and this, Kurozumi *Sensei*, is why it seemed very peculiar when you carefully took the smaller fish, one by one. Even if you had left the picking to the peddler, he would have mixed big ones in with the small ones to balance the sizes and get the price at the average for you.

But you have taken the trouble to choose the smaller ones on purpose. At any rate, if you don't mind my saying it, that was not reasonable of you. It was actually quite silly.

When his disciple was finished. *Kyōso* said.

Well, that is the point. I am always teaching. "When you are buying, put yourself in the position of the seller."

This is said to have been his reply.

VIII

A Rice Bowl and Floss Silk

Once *Kyōso* was giving lectures at a certain Buddhist temple.

Please, listen to me. When someone throws a rice bowl to you, don't try to catch it with another rice bowl. You should catch it softly with floss silk. In this way the rice bowl will not break or make a noise.

This is what he preached.

A man who was there listening to the lecture stood up and spoke in an accusing tone.

Sensei, are you sure that a rice bowl and floss silk will make no noise?

Kyōso answered,

I am positive they will make not a sound.

Then the man came nearer, and said even more excitedly,

Sir, are you definitely sure there will be no noise?

Hearing this, *Kyōso* responded calmly with a serene countenance,

Oh yes, my friend, the two will make a sound.

The man sat down again in his place satisfied, as if saying,

Didn't I tell you so?

So, here was a man who began by throwing a rice bowl. And, here *Kyōso* disregarded what he had just been saying and ignored reasonable thinking to say, "Yes, sir. You are right. The two will make a sound."

We see, however, that *Kyōso's* action in conceding to the listener was actually a vivid demonstration of catching a rice bowl with floss silk, as he had just been preaching.

IX

One Family at Peace and Another in Discord

1

Kyōso once gave a sermon as follows.

There was once a family that was well known for being very peaceful, and there was another that had the opposite reputation. A certain person was curious about that, and went to find out the reasons for the difference.

First he visited the peaceful family. When he entered the front garden of the house he saw the grandfather sitting down in the doorway and enjoying big puffs of tobacco after putting down in the inner garden a big pot he had just bought and taken home.

Not knowing the pot was there, his son threw down a bundle of firewood from the upper floor. The cracking noise of the pot told him what happened then. The son hurried down to his father and apologized humbly, bowing his head with his hands on the floor. The old man replied that it was his own fault, since he had put the pot down in a bad place.

Then his wife came, confessing that she should have put the pot away as soon as her husband came in and apologizing that she had not done it. The son's wife then came in, saying her mother-in-law's action was quite natural and she was not responsible since she hadn't known her son was upstairs. The young woman said that she herself should have put the pot away, because she had been aware of what was going on. She apologized that she had not been more thoughtful and careful.

Then the old man broke in, "No, no, it's not anybody's fault. Let's look at it this way. The bundle hit the pot and broke it, and so it did not land on my head as if to drive out an evil spirit. To our good fortune, no one was hurt. What could be better than that?"

With this the incident was settled in peace and harmony and no one was left with any blame.

2

Then the fellow went to the other house. As it happened, the grandfather of this home had just returned with a *shō* (about 1.8 liters) of sake in a sake bottle *(tokkuri)*. He put it down in the doorway and forgot it. Minutes later his son came in from the field and accidentally kicked the bottle over and broke it. He shouted loudly, saying it was the fault of whoever left it there. The old man came out and scolded his son, "You should have been more careful of where you were walking. You should have watched your steps."

Soon after that the grandmother chimed in, saying her husband was to blame because he had left the bottle in the doorway in the first place. Her words made the old man angry. "You should have been more careful. You should have put it away yourself." The old woman called in her daughter-in-law and complained that she was very old and couldn't see well. The younger woman was the one who should have put it away. The young woman answered back that she had been in the rear part of the house where she hadn't even known what was going on.

All of this started up a big and unpleasant quarrel, adding to the disagreements in the family.

In a peaceful family each member becomes the one at fault and takes the blame for things. Everything is settled in roundness, peace, and harmony.

But, in a family in discord, each member tries to look like the good person, taking liberties in trying to look better. In this way, everything ends with no meaning and no favorable outcome. Any good will that might have been there dies out for lack of encouragement.

X

Keeping His Promise with a Highwayman

1

The sun had already set and *Kyōso* was still walking home from some missionary work in Bitchū province (to the west of modern Okayama city). He was walking alone through a very lonesome area where there were no houses and no one else walking. The location was perhaps close to Yonekura, a hamlet a few kilometers from Kaminakano.

Suddenly a man jumped out from behind some shelter and stood in the middle of the road, blocking the way. He demanded, "I am in desperate need of ten *ryō*. Lend it to me or else!"

Fig. 17   The "hand-washing place" *(temizuya)* where the Founder buried money for the highwayman. Such places for purification are found at shrines everywhere in Japan. *Courtesy of Kurozumikyō.*

The fellow was a highwayman, a robber.

After hearing what he said, *Kyōso* looked closely at the robber for a moment and then calmly responded,

> Are you sure you by all means need the money? It does look like something has happened to you that leaves you no choice but to stop someone in the road and ask to borrow money.
>
> I would like to lend you what you are asking, but, unfortunately, I only have five *ryō* with me now. I am sorry, but for now please take what I have.
>
> As to the remaining five *ryō*, I will bury it in the ground beside the washing place[117] in front of the Imamura Shrine. I will leave a small stone there to mark where it is buried. Please be sure to come to the shrine tomorrow night and pick up the money. I assure you, you will find the five *ryō* buried where I said it would be.

2

The highwayman stood there for a while with nothing to say, staring back at *Kyōso*. Then he quickly said to himself,

> This old man looks very honest. But he might be good at telling lies. Still, he is very polite. When I demanded ten *ryō* he took that for serious truth. He gave me five *ryō* and promised to give me the rest tomorrow.

On one hand he was much impressed, and on the other, he was really puzzled by *Kyōso's* sincerity and uprightness.

When the robber showed up at the shrine the following night, half in doubt, the five *ryō* was there as he was told it would be. "After all the gentleman was truly honest. Today, there is nobody like this in the world." The fellow was much touched with *Kyōso's* sincerity and kindness, and at the same time he found himself feeling ashamed of his wretched heart and bad conduct.

It is said that before too long he joined in the pursuit of the Way to prove himself another faithful and devoted follower.

XI

The Story of the Cat that Fell in a Well

This happened when *Kyōso* was walking past Daiku on his way into Okayama on a religious mission. There was a big, excited gathering of people along the road just there, and he stopped to see what was happening.

With him was Hishikawa Ginjibei, his personal attendant. Looking more closely, *Kyōso* saw they were trying to rescue a poor cat that had fallen into a well.

When they lowered a bamboo basket tied to the end of a long piece of rope, the cat quickly got into the basket, as the old saying goes, "a drowning man will grab even a piece of straw." They carefully and slowly pulled up the rope to lift the basket, but when the basket was almost all the way up, the frightened cat tried to save itself by jumping out too soon, and fell back into the well with a splash.

They tried the same thing again, but when they were again about to succeed, the cat in its fear and haste did the same thing again. Their third and fourth attempts also ended the same way. The rescuers started mumbling to themselves about what a stupid brute the cat was. "What do you expect from such a dumb animal!" But the cat was showing signs of weakening.

It isn't clear at just what point *Kyōso's* eyes began filling with tears. Ginjibei, in his own straightforward way, urged him to keep walking, but he kept looking back. Suddenly *Kyōso* came to a stop, saying to himself with tears running down his cheeks, "Oh, my, what a pity and a sorrow!" Then Ginjibei grumbled,

It really was a sad scene, sure enough. But though it is a pitiful sight, it was only something happening to an animal. I don't think it is worth the *Sensei* crying over it.

Hearing this, *Kyōso* replied sharply,

Gin-san, you are wrong. It's not a matter of just a poor cat. It applies also to us humans. People might look intelligent and smart, but they keep on repeating the same mistakes. Kami is always stretching out her hands to us, trying hard in various ways to tell us, "Now is your time to be saved, now you will be cured." If only we had more patience and could keep from moving away from the help she is giving.

Alas! So quickly our selfish heart comes to the fore. We resort too soon to our smartness and cleverness. When that is the kind of effort we put forth, all we have gained is lost each time. We put ourselves deeper and deeper into a hole.

Oh, what frustrated and compassionate feelings Kami must have on seeing that happen. When I think about it this way, how can I keep my tears from falling?

Oh, our gracious Kami! Today again you have taught me a graceful and precious lesson. I extend my sincere and humble thanks to you.

XII

Okumura Enzaemon Regains His Eyesight

1

An incident that has some points in common with the story of the blessing of Ogata *sensei* (chapter 4) has been passed on to us to illustrate the greatest and most miraculous blessing of all.

A certain unfortunate blind man heard that regardless of the nature of the disease, all patients who visited Kurozumi *Sensei* of Kaminakano were blessed with recovery. The poor man decided to visit this gentleman with the desperate hope of getting his eyesight back. After his first visit, he attended every meeting held on the "two and seven" days of the month. He spent three full years attending and listening to *Kyōso's* gratifying lectures, receiving the *majinai* ritual after each meeting. But alas, he was still unable to see even a little glint of light.

2

When the meeting that marked the end of three full years of worshiping was almost over, the blind man waited until everyone had left and went to *Kyōso* to tell him his discouragement and disappointment.

Sir, I have come to be excused from your meetings and to bid you goodbye. That is why I stayed behind waiting for the last person to leave. Sir, it might seem strange to you, but since I started coming I have not missed a single meeting. But, to my disappointment, my eyes have received no blessing. Of course, I tried hard to understand what the Way is really about. I have personally observed that many have received boundless blessings in many different ways during this time. I want you to know I hold no doubt about that at all.

Sir, I have enjoyed the great pleasure and honor of receiving your personal *majinai* scores of times. But alas, my eyes are still as blind as they were three years ago. I cannot see even a slight glimmering of light. I am sure you will understand what a difficulty it is for a blind person to attend six meetings every month for three years. Please realize the efforts I devoted to fulfilling this desire of mine and the trouble I have gone to.

Sir, it may be that my faith is not enough. To my deepest regret, I can't think of anything more to be done. There is no way left but to give up all hope and to reconcile myself to my fate.

And sir, in this connection, I am afraid that if I keep on coming to your meetings it will hurt your reputation and virtue and may cause an obstacle in spreading the Way. Since I worry about such a result, I will stop attending any more. From this day I ask your permission to be excused from the meetings.

He was finding difficulty in expressing himself, and uttered his words in a grief-stricken, inconsolable way. His seriousness reflected vividly his poor inner soul.

3

Kyōso, who was listening quietly to what the man said, suddenly clapped his hands graciously.

Oh, what an immense and abundant blessing you have received! How fortunate you are and how grateful you should be!

The poor man was taken aback by these words, and responded in confusion and with some heat.

Sir, oh no, no. I said there were no blessings.

Restraining him, *Kyōso* said,

Don't you know what you are saying? Think what you have been doing. Six times a month means you have gone to the trouble of attending more than two hundred meetings, not missing even one.

Throughout these three years you were never ill, never suffered a stomachache, not even a cold. More than that, you never had to stay home in bed. That is because you spent three full years enjoying a perfect state of health. Isn't that evidence of plentiful blessings?

Besides that, it wasn't only you. No member of your family was sick. Otherwise there would have been times you could not come. Bear in mind that you were able to attend every meeting without any hindrance or obstacle of that sort.

Oh, and beyond that. If someone in your family had passed away during this time, or a relative living close to you or far away, it would have kept you from attending. That would have been a source of taboo, keeping you from going out to shrines or to all sorts of events.[118]

So, in spite of all such things that might have happened, you were still able to attend all the meetings, every five days, all six meetings each month. What a gracious blessing you have received!

With this, *Kyōso* again clapped his hands.

4

The blind man was deeply moved by this explanation. He had listened quietly, and was struck by the sharp sound of *Kyōso's* handclap as if hit by lightning.

Oh, sir, I was mistaken. Thank you so much.

His words half finished, he ran to the doorway leaving behind the walking cane he had been using. With swinging steps he walked out of *Kyōso's* place. Touched with indescribably strong gratitude and deep emotion, he passed Niwaseguchi, Kawaramachi-suji, then Saidaichō, and found himself crossing Kyōbashi bridge over the Asahi river. At this moment he felt a cool river breeze. He thought,

Oh, I am crossing a river. Where could this be?

Then he looked around. The spacious scene of the Asahi river, and all of the ships coming in and going out and those in the harbor, came into his eyes.

Oh, how wonderful! I can see with my own eyes! They are open! I've recovered my sight!

His voice was a sound coming up from the depth of his heart. The words coming out of his mouth were uttered so innocently, they were so spontaneous and pure, so firm, the most joyful and most grateful that any human being could ever pronounce.

The person in this anecdote is reportedly Okumura Enzaemon, a Bizen samurai who entered the faith in 1845.

XIII

The Lesson of the Live and Dead Twigs

This is an anecdote from a sermon given at a meeting.

The other day I happened to look out and see many children flying kites high up in the sky, and I learned a lesson from Kami for which I am very thankful. Now and then a kite would be caught on the twigs and branches of trees. One boy pulled with all his might to release his kite.

Watching carefully, I saw that most of the kites that got caught on live twigs remained intact and uncut, and could be gotten off easily. But those that got caught on dead twigs and branches were hard to get free and could hardly be saved. Such efforts mostly ended up in cutting the string and losing the kite.

With this, I came to have a new understanding. When our hearts are vigorous and active, communication with others goes along smoothly and every problem gets a clear solution easily.

On the other hand, when your heart is dead or inactive and you feel gloomy, anything that comes up provokes a problem, and the whole thing becomes more and more complicated. Everything gets all tangled up, going haywire and causing a great mess, leading to an unsolvable commotion. You damage parts of the kite or you fail to recover the string and the kite from the twig and the branch. What a mess this is!

This is exactly the Way of the Great Kami: reviving a person's heart with the living divine heart. There is no other way than this.

I had watched the children playing, but what a great and gracious lesson I learned from Heaven, in accordance with the rule of Nature. Oh Kami, thank you so much!

XIV

The Benefits and Virtues Realized through Laughter

1

There was a patient living in the city of Okayama who had been suffering a serious case of tuberculosis. *Kyōso* was invited to his place to perform a ritual of *majinai* on him. After the ritual *Kyōso* told him,

I am sorry to say it, but I have been thinking ever since I got here that this room is very gloomy. It is natural that your illness would have that result, and that your heart is gloomy with all your troubles and difficulties. And the members of your family also are in a gloomy and dark mood all the time. Furthermore, the doors and *shōji* screens are kept closed, making the room even darker. It is full of gloominess.

Although your situation is understandable and reasonable, gloominess is taboo for one devoted in faith. Vitalizing your life is the divine way of things. Enjoying your life is the divine way, complying with the holy heart of the Great Kami. Please, try to get a spark of cheerfulness into yourself.

The first thing you should do is to laugh. It looks like you have not laughed for years. From this very day, try to laugh as much and as often as possible.

The man replied,

Thank you, sir. But, it is hard for me to laugh. I am not in a mood for it. How can I laugh?

Kyōso returned,

I can only say, "Try to laugh. Do your best." Although you have no reason to laugh you should try anyhow. You might just have to do it on purpose. Open your mouth wide open, and say, "ha, ha, ha."

The man responded,

I am sure that is quite simple and easy for you.

All through the night the patient kept pondering this.

To laugh on purpose might not be so hard. I think I could do that. If it really would relieve me of my illness, it would be an easy way to be cured.

He started trying to laugh. But since he felt nothing to laugh at he found no joy in it. He thought how ridiculous it was even to try. With reluctance, again and again, he tried to laugh. "Ha, ha, ha."

Then he happened to notice that the paper-covered lantern was reflecting his shadow on the *shōji* screen. His face was gaunt and rawboned, no flesh was left on his cheeks, and his mouth was moving in an awkward way as he seriously tried with all his might to laugh. It dawned on him how grotesque his shadow was looking. It was extremely funny, suddenly he saw how comic it was! No one would be able to keep from laughing!

It was an unexpected experience for him, after trying on purpose to laugh for no reason at all. Spontaneously, he burst into real laughter. The humor was suddenly more than he could hold in. For some moments his sides were shaking with merriment.

The unusual sound woke up the members of his family who came running to his room. The story and the funny shadow made them all laugh. Of course, the patient was in turn provoked to join them in even more laughter. Their sides were shaking with laughter, all of them.

2

The laughing he had not enjoyed for years relieved him of the congestion of blood in his stomach. His blood circulation showed sudden improvement. With his abdominal muscles activated, his appetite was enhanced and he began to feel hungry. Best of all, all gloominess had faded away and he felt happy and joyful.

Although he ate only a little at his next meal, he ate it with a hearty appetite. That night he sank into a deep and profound sleep such as he had been missing for years. His condition improved from the following morning on, and eventually he was able to overcome the incurable disease.

It was indeed a blessing of *"warai-harai,"* "laughing-purification," because the patient was able to purify himself through laughter.

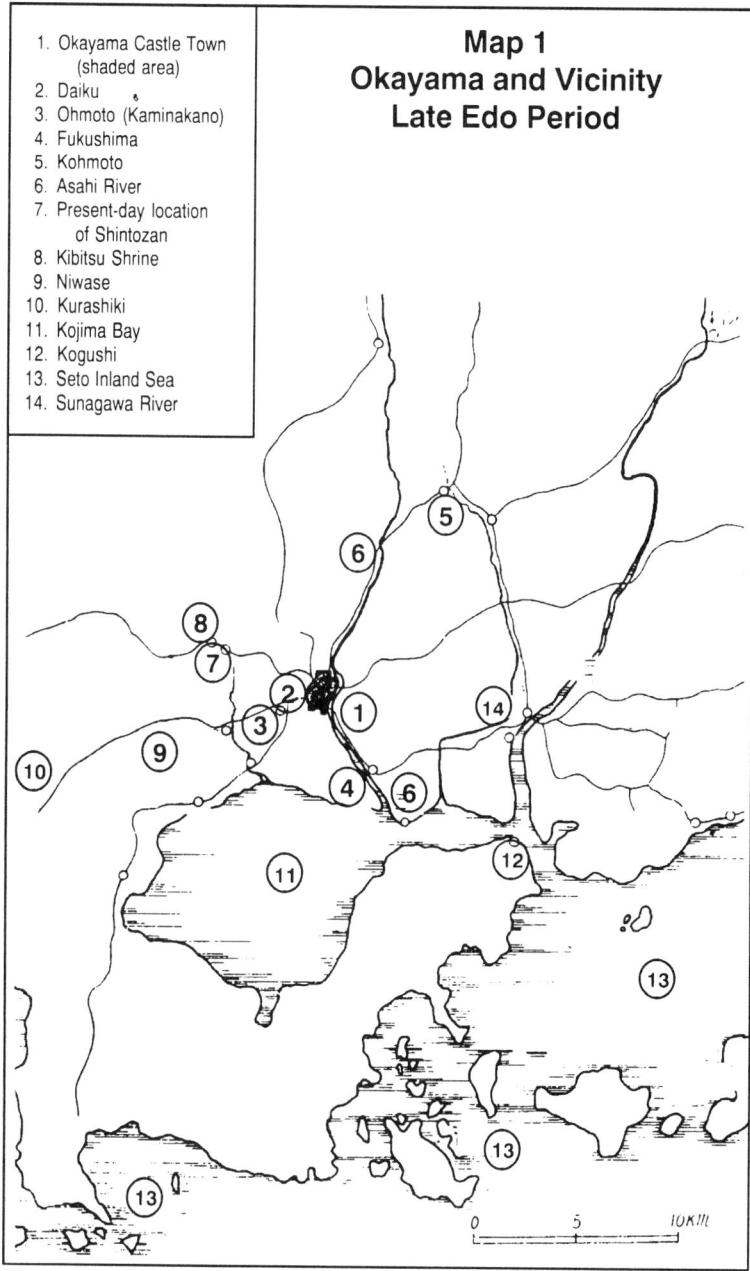

1. Okayama Castle Town
   (shaded area)
2. Daiku
3. Ohmoto (Kaminakano)
4. Fukushima
5. Kohmoto
6. Asahi River
7. Present-day location
   of Shintozan
8. Kibitsu Shrine
9. Niwase
10. Kurashiki
11. Kojima Bay
12. Kogushi
13. Seto Inland Sea
14. Sunagawa River

**Map 1
Okayama and Vicinity
Late Edo Period**

0   5   10 KM.

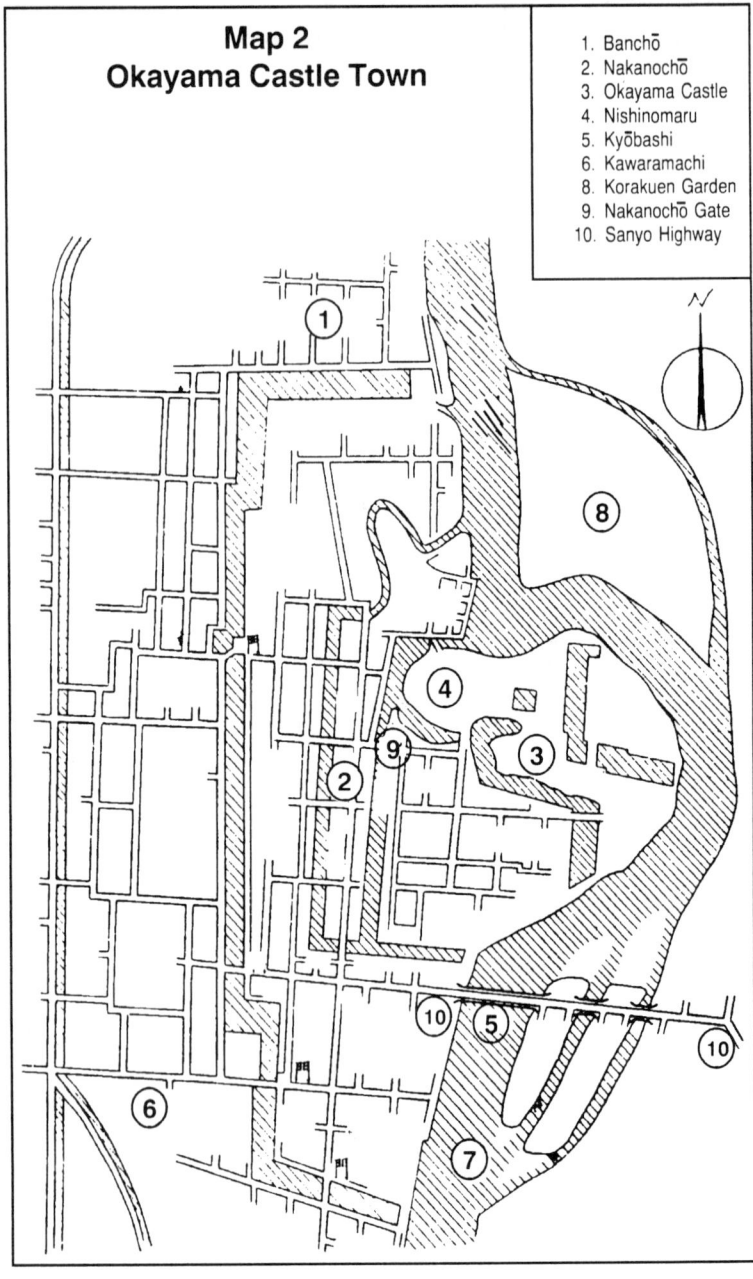

Map 2
Okayama Castle Town

1. Banchō
2. Nakanochō
3. Okayama Castle
4. Nishinomaru
5. Kyōbashi
6. Kawaramachi
8. Korakuen Garden
9. Nakanochō Gate
10. Sanyo Highway

Notes

[1] Willis Stoesz, ed., *Kurozumi Shinto; an American Dialogue* (Chambersburg: Anima Publications, 1989).

[2] A convenient summary of Shinto is given by H. Byron Earhart in Stoesz, ed., *Kurozumi Shinto*, 11-27. For fuller discussion see Sokyo Ono, *Shinto; the Kami Way* (Rutland: Charles E. Tuttle & Co., 1962) and Joseph Kitigawa, *On Understanding Japanese Religion* (Princeton: Princeton University Press, 1987), 139-173.

[3] See especially Joseph Kitagawa, *Religion in Japanese History* (New York: Columbia University Press, 1966) and Murakami Shigeyoshi, *Japanese Religion in the Modern Period,* trans. H. Byron Earhart (Tokyo: Tokyo University Press, 1980).

[4] See Helen Hardacre, *Shinto and the State, 1868-1988* (Princeton: Princeton University Press, 1989), for the most authoritative and recent account.

[5] Belief in *ikigami* occurred also amid the turbulent social phenomena connected with the Ise pilgrimage, as part of the hope many common people felt for world-renewal. Winston Davis, *Japanese Religion and Society; Paradigms of Structure and Change* (Albany: State University of New York Press, 1992), 59. Though Munetada went on this pilgrimage six times and lectured about it for years, his personal development was marked by high ethical concern and respect for local governing authorities. His position as priest in a local shrine gave him a stability many others involved in the pilgrimage, such as the agents of the Ise Shrine and, especially, the many self-appointed provocateurs and seekers of gain and fame, did not have.

He differed also from high-minded people of the times who sought to renew the world through direct action. See Irwin Scheiner, "Benevolent Lords and Honorable Peasants: Rebellion and Peasant Consciousness in Tokugawa Japan," in Tetsuo Najita and Irwin Scheiner, *Japanese Thought in the Tokugawa Period* (Chicago: University of Chicago Press, 1978), 39-62. Munetada sought no redress of grievances for perceived social ills; the renewal he experienced himself and sought for in others was focussed in the inner spirit and promoted health and harmony.

[6] The details of his development, from dutiful son seeking excellence in Confucian virtues so as to be a great credit to his parents, to becoming a founder of a new departure in Japanese religion based on his own transformative, ecstatic union with Amaterasu, are discussed in Willis Stoesz, "The Universal Attitude of Kurozumi Munetada," in Stoesz, ed., *Kurozumi Shinto,* 115-134.

[7] Alan Miller has made the intriguing suggestion that Munetada's two-part vow resembles the Buddhist concept of the bodhisattva vow, fundamental to Mahayana Buddhism. Alan Miller, "Internalization of Kami: Buddhist affinities in Kurozumi-kyō," in Stoesz, ed., *Kurozumi Shinto,* 135-155. However, it is not that he thought of himself as a Buddhist or was so regarded by others, but that elements in Japanese culture originating in that tradition came together in his vow-action in a way similar to Buddhism. His vow was Shinto in form and resembled Buddhism in substance, particularly in its compassionate tone and as he understood his ecstatic union with Amaterasu in "non-dual" language. As Helen

Hardacre has pointed out, Munetada probably had become familiar with that language through the Neo-Confucian-oriented Shingaku movement founded by Ishida Baigan (1685-1744). Helen Hardacre, *Kurozumikyōand the New Religions of Japan* (Princeton: Princeton University Press, 1986), 47. Kurozumikyō understands the compassion of Munetada to be directed toward all universally; and we see that Shinto religion draws on a broad cultural tradition. See the comment by the Reverend Kurozumi Muneharu, "The Teaching of Kurozumi-kyō" in Stoesz, ed., *Kurozumi Shinto*, 49-65. Japanese religion, particularly in the pre-Meiji era, displays a coming-together of motifs that historians of religion may separate for purposes of analytic understanding.

[8] Munetada's state of enlightenment *(issai shintoku kan)* is comparable to Buddhist *satori,* but emphasizes utter reliance on divine virtue in a way that Zen, at least, does not. References to the "non-dual" state of mind abound in his writing.

[9] "Creator" does not mean *creatio ex nihilo* as in western religions, making the world from nothing at the beginning of time. In keeping with Japanese mythological belief, the origination of all kami within time is assumed. The emphasis in the concept is on the creation of each moment's goodness and harmony, as people sincerely rely on her inner presence.

[10] For more discussion of the distinction between "insiders" and "outsiders" in the study of Kurozumi Shinto see Stoesz, ed., *Kurozumi Shinto, passim.*

[11] See Hardacre, *Kurozumikyō and the New Religions of Japan*, 42ff. For a description of the Okayama area see Richard Beardsley et al., *Village Japan* (Chicago: The University of Chicago Press, 1959). Several of Munetada's closest followers were recognized scholars.

[12] Davis, *Japanese Religion and Society.* For an indication of Munetada's approach to such issues, see the story of the upset doll stand given in the Appendix (Story Four).

[13] Charles W. Hepner, *The Kurozumi Sect of Shintō,* (Tokyo: Meiji Japan Society, 1935).

[14] Nobuhara Taisen, *The Brilliant Life of Munetada Kurozumi; a Philosopher and Worshipper of the Sun,* trans. Sakai Tsukasa and Sasage Kazuko, 2nd revision (Tokyo: PMC Publications, Inc., 1982).

[15] Hardacre, *Kurozumikyō and the New Religions of Japan.* The term "core values" is from Robert Bellah, *Tokugawa Religion; the Cultural Roots of Modern Japan* (New York and London: The Free Press, 1985. Orig. 1957).

[16] Preparation of an English edition of the complete collection of the stories of the Founder *(itsuwa)* is under way, with Kamiya Sumio doing the translating and Willis Stoesz editing the translation.

[17] Before Japan's adoption of the western Gregorian calendar in 1873 the Japanese calendar followed a complicated system based on Chinese tradition and on the agricultural cycle. It involved the occasional use of intercalary months, so that dates often correspond only roughly and with varying closeness to modern calendar dates. For this reason dates before that year are given in the Japanese manner: "first day of the third month," etc. See the helpful article on "Calendar" in the *Encyclopedia of Japan.*

[18] A period when there were two emperors began in 1336 when the Ashikaga Shogun seized power in Kyōto by installing a member of the imperial family of

their choice, so that the existing Emperor Go-Daigo fled to Yoshino, south of Nara, and set up the "Southern Court." The dispute was settled in 1392. See George Sansom, *Japan: A Short Cultural History*, 2nd rev. ed, (Stanford: Stanford University Press, 1978), 351ff.

[19] Hachiman is a Kami dating to ancient times and has a general importance throughout Japanese tradition. Numerous old shrines dedicated to him are found throughout Japan. He is associated with warlike qualities. For information on the Hachiman tradition see Christine Kanda, *Shinzo: Hachiman Imagery and its Development* (Cambridge: Harvard University Press, 1985).

[20] However, the Kurozumi family, serving as priests, did not receive a stipend from the government *(han)*, as did the samurai who were on permanent retainer to the governing feudal family.

[21] The Munetada Shrine was constructed in 1879, next to the house built for the Founder in 1848.

[22] Hardacre notes that a *negi* is an assistant in ritual, ranked neither the highest nor the lowest among priests of a local shrine. Hardacre, *Kurozumikyō and the New Religions of Japan*, 50n.

[23] Tanuma Okitsugu served as senior councillor during the reign of Shogun Ieharu (1760-1786), holding near-dictatorial power as he sought to cure the economic ills of the country while also advancing his family's financial fortunes. A general decline in public morale resulted. See Mikiso Hane, *Modern Japan; a Historical Survey* (Boulder: Westview Press, 1986), 42f., for further details.

[24] For details see John W. Hall, *Government and Local Power in Japan* (Princeton: Princeton University Press, 1966). Economic and social changes in the late Edo period were putting many people under strain; see Susan Hanley and Kozo Yamamura, *Economic and Demographic Change in Preindustrial Japan* (Princeton: Princeton University press, 1977), 161-198, for an account of these trends. For a general discussion of the problems this created for ordinary people, see Anne Walthall, *Social Protest and Popular Culture in Eighteenth-Century Japan* (Tucson: University of Arizona Press, 1986). For a discussion of the intellectual climate in Japanese culture at the time, including the Okayama area, see the essays in Peter Nosco, ed., *Confucianism and Tokugawa Culture* (Princeton: Princeton University Press, 1984).

[25] Hereafter these two sources will be cited as *Short Biography* and *Biography* respectively.

[26] References to the *Tales of the Founder* will be by the number assigned them in the published edition. See the Bibliography, Part I, for further explanation.

[27] See R.P. Dore, *Education in Tokugawa Japan* (Berkeley: University of California Press, 1965), for a description of the kind of schools available for children's education at the time.

[28] "Kami" has a wide range of meanings, most often referring to any of a wide range of spirits, or spiritual presences, but occasionally referring to such divine qualities as harmony, purity and truth. When the term is capitalized it refers to a kami of central importance, such as Amaterasu.

To aspire to become a kami-like person, a "living kami," is to aspire to a very high spiritual condition. Through his intense religious practice and through subsequent events in his personal life, Munetada became a person of considerable spiritual power. As Founder of Kurozumikyō he is himself venerated as a Kami.

See Helen Hardacre, *Kurozumikyō and the New Religions of Japan*, 52f. and Stoesz, ed., *Kurozumi Shinto*, 52ff, 272.

[29] In the Confucian tradition Heaven *(Ten)* is a universal moral presence and source of order in human life and in nature, sometimes referred to in broadened terms as Heaven and Earth *(Tenchi;* "Universe"). To listen to the inner bidding is to be attentive to the universal principle of order as perceived within one's self. It is an idea as old as the *Analects* of Confucius, but given deepened emphasis in Neo-Confucianism in its concept of the microcosmic inner principle *(li)*. See Wm. Theodore de Bary and Irene Bloom, eds., *Principle and Practicality; Essays in Neo-Confucianism and Practical Learning* (New York: Columbia University Press, 1979), for extensive discussion of this central concept.

In Munetada's mature thought, Heaven also expresses itself in personalized terms as Amaterasu Ōmikami, the Sun Kami. His warm personal piety toward her is focused through the morning sunrise service, where she is understood thereby to become active in the body of the Kurozumikyō worshipper in a kind of sacrament. She is present within each person as a "divided portion" *(bunshin)*, a "living-thing" *(ikimono)*, just as she is also present in the universe as a whole *(honshin)*.

[30] Texts for the Noh theatre date from the 14th century C.E. and are highly formal and poetic. Performances of Noh drama were familiar in Okayama; the nearby Kibitsu shrine, for instance, has a stage that was used for the purpose. Individuals committed to a Confucian ideal of personal culture might learn to chant them as a form of private enjoyment and personal development. Their content is deeply Buddhist, with a powerful sense of the destiny (karma; Japanese *innen*) the characters in the dramas have earned by their actions. See Donald Keene, *World Within Walls* (New York: Holt, Rinehart, and Winston, 1976) for a discussion of the cultured literary world of the times.

[31] See Chapter 5 for a list of the six pilgrimages Munetada undertook. The Reverend Kurozumi Munetada notes that the founder's understanding of his purpose in doing them went through a change. In the first he had in mind worshiping the Amaterasu of traditional mythology, ancestress of the Imperial family. After the intervening experience of his enlightenment, however, she had for him a universal meaning as he undertook the remaining five. Kurozumi Muneharu, "Kurozumi-kyō in Japanese Culture," in Stoesz, ed., *Kurozumi Shinto*, 92-101; see especially 95f.

[32] A list of all Kurozumi documents is given in the Bibliography.

[33] *"Satori"* is a term often associated in English with Buddhist enlightenment, but it is a common term in Japanese for many kinds of comprehension, mental clarification, insight, etc. It occurs often in Kurozumi Tadaaki's text of the *Kysōden*, but in this translation the word "enlightenment" is used only to refer to Munetada's definitive experience of unity with Amaterasu Ōmikami referred to as the Direct Bestowal of Divine Mission (Chapter 3). "This standpoint is what we refer to as *Issai-shintoku-kan: "Issai,"* all [-encompassing], *"shintoku,"* "Divine Blessings or Virtues," and *"kan,"* "view, or outlook." "It is to look at or on everything from the grateful standpoint of the fundamental recognition of Divine Virtue." (Personal correspondence from The Reverend Kurozumi Tadaaki, July 3, 1993). *"Issai-shintoku-kan"* thus is the viewpoint of enlightenment resulting from the Direct Bestowal of Divine Mission, the mandate on which Munetada's life was

thereafter based. "Fulfillment" here translates *mi wo musubu.* Thanks to Professor Harold Wright who assisted me in sorting out the nuances of a number of passages in the book where the term *satori* in its nominal and verbal forms occurred.

[34] As Hardacre points out, he was here vowing to become a healing kami *(reijin),* one excelling in communication between humans and the spirit world. A different kind of kami is here in view than was involved in being a "living kami" *(ikigami).* Later, the two forms both became part of his identity as the Founder Kami, a distinctive new development in Japanese spirituality. Cp. Hardacre, *Kurozumikyōand the New Religions of Japan,* 48, 52.

[35] Three special occasions of sun worship *(nippai),* called *Gohai,* were turning points as Munetada went from severe illness to the enlightened condition in which he was the Founder. Such worship of the sun was a traditional form of piety, to which Munetada's distinctive experience gave the rich meaning with which Kurozumikyō still observes this ritual central to its life.

[36] The *Gokōden* is a summary of a longer work *(Gokōshakuden)* which contains stories about the Founder recounted by people who had been in direct contact with him and who retold these stories in their teaching.

[37] *Gobun* are letters written by the Founder to his followers. They are collected as Part Two of the *Kurozumikyō Kyōsho,* the official compilation of the teachings of Kurozumikyō.

[38] "Clouds" is a metaphor for fault, or moral shortcoming. "Sin" in the Christian sense would be too strong a word for the milder Shinto sense of moral fault.

[39] *Goshinryo* here implies a commitment or intention at the foundation of the universe ("Heaven," or "Heaven-and-Earth"), "within its inner heart," toward the harmony and well being of all who are in the universe. The Kami Amaterasu expresses this intention, so that it may be understood as love or desire for that harmony. It is not far removed from the concepts of "vow" or "promise."

[40] *Enrei Hi wo morashi*
Zoka no hei wo nigirashimu.
Author's note: "Handle" does not refer specifically to the staff in the founder's hand, but rather to his ability to act in expression of the spirit of the Round Spirit. See Figure 12.

[41] *Go* is a familiar game in Japan, similar to chess but played with small black and white stones identical in size.

[42] Those taking part in Kurozumi morning sun worship *(nippai)* take in air through the mouth at the moment the sun rises, thus taking in the light at the same time. In this way they follow the example of Munetada the Founder at his Third Gohai, at which the bestowal of identity with Amaterasu occurred. The presence of Amaterasu herself, expressed as divine energy *(yōki),* is communicated by this inrush of grace-laden breath. See Stoesz, ed., *Kurozumi Shinto,* 70f.

[43] Events referred to as *kinen* ("memorable events") were occasions when healing grace was directly received. These faith healings were a "marvel" *(majinai)* to those who were affected. We will use the term untranslated.

[44] I.e., free of *Ki sho ten ketsu,* the formal introduction and conclusion used in Chinese literature. He understood his words to be *"ukabi no mama no,"* floating up into the mind "just as they are," intact. His inner spirit had returned to the state of purity the human spirit originally had in creation, free of any admixture of self-will *(ga).*

[45] The "divided portion" *(miwaketama)* is the inner presence of Amaterasu within the spirit *(kokoro)* of every human being. The Reverend Kurozumi Tadaaki comments, "We, mankind, are Divine Children of Amaterasu, and are all blessed with *bunshin.* As long as we are awakened with and are aware of the *miwaketama* and cultivate our hearts, never to offend the Divine Soul or Will, no doubt exists whatsoever of failure. Without any fear, all effort will surely prove rewarding. This view is *shinjin funi kan (shin,* or kami; *jin,* or *hito,* man; *kan,* or view); namely, the recognition that god and mankind are in oneness and [having a] standpoint on this basis" (Personal correspondence, July 3, 1993).

[46] Translation by Kamiya Sumio.

[47] English version by the editor.

[48] *Ikidōshi,* literally, "living through," is the Founder's term for the ideal human condition. All aspects of a living person are harmoniously integrated in each moment of time, the wholeness of the cosmos as a whole being bestowed by virtue of Amaterasu's presence, now indwelling fully in an individual person. She is the *honshin,* the universal spirit, who in *ikidōshi* is in each moment fully one with the *bunshin,* the inner "separate" spirit of a person. To know Amaterasu is to be undying; that is, ordinary death is not a problem to a person with abiding life. It is a condition of the utmost happiness.

I am indebted to Harold Wright for suggesting this phrase to translate *ikidōshi.*

[49] In Shinto worship the clap of the hands, most often twice, is an expression of reverent attention recognizing the presence of a kami. As Hardacre suggests, it is like calling out "Amen!" at a Christian service of worship. Hardacre, *Kurozumikyō and the New Religions of Japan,* 71.

[50] Author's note: The metaphor suggests that while the pestle (the Founder) is the instrument by which rice is pounded to be cleaned, the grains of rice also rub against each other, assisting and completing the cleaning process.

[51] For a discussion of the use of charms and amulets in Kurozumikyō, see Eugene Swanger, *"Omamori* in Kurozumikyō," in Stoesz, ed., *Kurozumi Shinto,* 182-191.

[52] *Monjin* is a traditional Japanese term for someone initiated into the inner circle of a teacher, such as a master weaver or a philosopher, to be closely schooled in the distinctive insights or skills of the master.

[53] *Sensei* is the ordinary term in Japanese for "teacher." Here we use it untranslated and capitalized in order to designate the Founder in his exceptional teaching role. All of the pledges cited were made to Amaterasu by way of Kurozumi *Sensei,* who himself had experienced being "pledged," or "dedicated," as he gained his divine mission in the Third Gohai experience. The Founder sets the example, leads the way, and teaches how to follow in order to gain the same unity with Amaterasu he himself had gained. He is the *misebumi,* the pathfinder. We may use the lower case *"sensei"* to refer to other recognized teachers.

[54] The term *michizure* is commonly used: "followers," or, more literally, "way-companions."

[55] A *koku* is a measure equal to a little more than five U.S. bushels. Payment to samurai in service to their feudal lords was made in *koku* of rice. The more *koku* of rice being paid, the higher rank the samurai in question.

[56] See Note 30.

[57] Ginjibei was not accorded the title of teacher or disciple, but was respected as a unique and virtuous older man.

[58] *Monjin nadokori ki, The Names and Addresses of Disciples.*

[59] See Okada Takehiko, "Neo-Confucian Thinkers in Nineteenth-Century Japan," in Peter Nosco, ed., *Confucianism and Tokugawa Culture* (Princeton: Princeton University Press, 1984), 215-250, for information on these and other Neo-Confucian scholars during this period. See also Tetsuo Najita, *Visions of Virtue in Tokugawa Japan* (Chicago: University of Chicago Press, 1987), 292ff.

[60] The traditional Japanese historical record is given in the honorific titles given to the reigns of emperors. In this translation these are omitted unless, as here, the title indicates some special characteristic of the years in question.

[61] His books relating to Kurozumikyō are:
Biography of the Great Deity Munetada (Munetada Daimyōjin Godenki)
Book of the Reverent Observance of the Divine Mission (Shijun Tenmei no Maki)
The Teachings of the Substitute Instructor (Daishi no Setsu)
Outline for Initiation (Nyumon Taii)
Outline of the Way (Dōtai Taii)
Outline of the Deity's Accomplishments (Shinseki Taii)
(These last three are known collectively as the "Three Outlines" *(San Taii).*
Prides of the Way (Michi no Hokori)
Texts for a Mission (Dendo Shimpen)

[62] Last two lines emended by the Editor.

[63] *I.e., shugyō.* Japanese culture is rich in many kinds of ascetic practices and other disciplines used to develop the inner spirit.

[64] *Kaiun* implies an opening, a clearing of the way, a beginning of development of good fortune and well-being. It does not mean the same as "luck," since that would omit the guiding presence of Amaterasu and faith in the underlying order and unity of all existence. It is a vigorous term used frequently in Kurozumikyō.

[65] The reference is to a non-dual "frame of mind" or attitude unconditioned by any polarities imposed in the mind by attachment to particulars. Yet the experience to which it refers also suggests a plenitude of well-being greater than any single form of expression this attitude or frame of mind can take.

[66] *Ikimono*, "living-thing," is a term Munetada frequently uses to refer to the presence of Amaterasu Ōmikami, working within the inner mind or heart. Amaterasu is also alternatively referred to as Heaven, or Heaven and Earth, or the Parent of Heaven and Earth, depending on mood or context. This shifting of terms of reference allows a broad flexibility in Munetada's expression of religious feeling. See Hardacre, *Kurozumikyō and the New Religions of Japan*, 53f., for further discussion.

[67] The author points out that this poem *(uta, or O-uta)*, parallels a poem by the founder of Shingon Buddhism, Kobo Daishi (774-835), who says of his mountain retreat:
Koya-san waiting,
    Darkness and serenity,
        for daylight to break
Dimly lighted by the torch
    Teaching Buddha's wisdom,

and another by Nichiren Shonin (1222-1282), founder of the Nichiren tradition in Japanese Buddhism:

> In this darkling world
> when the moon is out of sight
> awaiting sunrise
> I shall be the saving guide
> leading everyone to light.

(The translations are by Kamiya Sumio.) The poem thus expresses the Founder's consciousness that his own experience, centered in morning *nippai*, especially that of the Third *Gohai* resulting in his Divine Mission, was the starting point of the Great Way. He understood that he was a Founder. *Uta* 133 has been revised slightly from Harold Wright's translation to bring this point out more clearly. Cp. Stoesz, ed., *Kurozumi Shinto*, 109.

We note, incidentally, that while the Founder designated some of his *uta* as teaching poems *(dōka)*, not all of them were so designated, including this one.

⁶⁸ *Makoto*, "sincerity," (*ch'eng* in Chinese) is a fundamental virtue in the Confucian ethical system that pervades Japanese culture. Heart-felt fidelity to one's self and to one's role in relation to others is its basic keynote. See, for instance, Julia Ching, *To Acquire Wisdom; The Way of Wang Yang-ming* (New York: Columbia University press, 1976), 200f.

⁶⁹ *Yamabushi*, mountain ascetics and wandering faith healers, have been part of the religious scene in Japan since early historic times. See Carmen Blacker, *The Catalpa Bow* (London: Geo. Allen & Unwin, 1975). Part of the time they were in residence in their mountain retreats, at other times they travelled about healing as needed, and sometimes they took up continuing residence in some village or neighborhood. Often they claimed a proprietary interest in some locality.

⁷⁰ *Den gobun* are those letters of the Founder that survive only as copies made by his followers.

⁷¹ *Haori* and *hakama*.

⁷² The Kurozumi family crest *(kamon)* was at shoulder height on the back of Munetada's *haori*, worn over the *kimono* and *hakama*. The Founder is regarded as the pathfinder *(misebumi)*, and the religious meaning of the story is clear to the reader.

⁷³ These can be found in Numbers 1 and 24 of the *Kyōsozasshu*, the *Miscellany* section of the Kurozumi scripture.

⁷⁴ Miscellany #46. *"Beniya"* indicates a merchant who was a dealer in rouge.

⁷⁵ *Maru kyō no shirushi*.

⁷⁶ For discussion of this practice *(sennichi sanro)*, see Hardacre, *Kurozumikyō and the New Religions of Japan*, 59f.; also given in Stoesz, ed., *Kurozumi Shinto*, 37ff. A common saying had it that "The words are easy to say, but it is hard to accomplish what they mean" (author's note). The visit to a hundred shrines was accomplished once a month for a period of nearly three years.

⁷⁷ Author's note: The *O Harai no Kotoba*, "Great Prayer of Purification," traditionally was chanted during two seasons of the year, at the end of June and of December, since earliest times. The Founder, however, chanted it many times at a sitting, at any time of the year, as an act of inner purification and to accompany

majinai. See also the comments by Kurozumi Muneharu in Stoesz, ed., *Kurozumi Shinto,* 67.; see also Hardacre, *Kurozumikyō and the New Religions of Japan,* 57ff.
[78] The "burning house" story is a familiar parable in the Lotus Sutra, a very familiar Buddhist scripture in Japanese history. See George J. Tanabe, Jr. and Willa Jane Tanabe, eds., *The Lotus Sutra in Japanese Culture* (Honolulu: University of Hawaii Press, 1989), for discussions of its immense significance.
[79] Translated by Helen Hardacre, *Kurozumikyō and the New Religions of Japan,* 67-68. Rule 2 has been edited by the author. The mood of these principles is somewhere between prescriptive and diagnostic, given as they are by the Founder as a guide to individual practice. The translation by Hepner, *The Kurozumi Sect of Shinto,* 159ff., may be consulted to note this contrast:

1.   Born in the Land of the Gods, and yet constantly without faith.
2.   The matter of getting Angry, and causing Pain to things.
3.   The matter of Self-Pride, which looks down on other people.
4.   The matter of strengthening one's Evil Purposes, by observing the Evil of others.
5.   The matter of neglecting one's Occupation when not ill.
6.   The matter of being in the True Way, without having Truth in the Heart.
7.   The matter failing to realize the things for which we should be daily Thankful.

On the development of the Five Principles into the list of Seven, see the discussion in Stoesz, ed., *Kurozumi Shinto,* 248.
[80] When one does not stick to one's basic idea, then one relative thought leads to another relative thought, making unstable the outer manifestation of the inner presence of Amaterasu Ōmikami.
[81] In becoming one with Kami, an individual may become kami.
[82] "Thank you" translates *"Arigatai"* rather weakly. Something like "wonderful!" "how rare!" "I am full of gratitude!" is suggested by this use of the term. It is in fact an ecstatic utterance distinctive to Kurozumikyō spirituality. I am indebted to Professor Kimiyuki Nishide for this suggestion.
[83] Author's note: the reference is to Confucianism.
[84] See Richard K. Beardsley, *et al., Village Japan,* for a description of the ancient and historic Kibi region.
[85] Author's note: Roundness, *maruki,* means perfection, integrity, endlessness, and infinity (being unconditioned). *Marukoto* ("round thing," or "matter" and *ikidōshi* ("abiding life") are very close in meaning.
[86] *Ukiyo,* in Munetada's hands, suggests something like "this worldly life;" it does not have specific reference to the "floating world" of the entertainment quarters of Edo period cities, as discussed, for instance, in George Sansom, *A Short Cultural History* (Stanford: Stanford University Press, 1978), 477ff. The fourth line has been emended by the editor.
[87] Edo, present-day Tokyo, is a very long way from Bizen, present-day Okayama, but that makes no difference as both find their true place in the one heart of Amaterasu through morning prayer before the sun. His implied wish for their good fortune and for being sustained in a far place by the love of Kami would be understood by the recipients of the letters. Emended by the editor.

[88] *Kegare,* pollution, is in Kurozumi Shinto expressed in terms of the inner spirit, and is not determined in its meaning by physical conditions as in traditional Shinto. See the comments on purity by Hajime Nakamura, *Ways of Thinking of Eastern Peoples* (Honolulu: University of Hawaii Press, 1964), 556. Davis connects the removal of *kegare* with world-renewal, *Japanese Religion and Society,* 76ff., an insight almost identical to what Munetada is here saying.
The distinction between *yōki* and *inki* derives from the yang-yin distinction in Taoism. However, the two are in Kurozumi piety not seen in naturalistic terms as in Taoism; *yōki* is an ideal to be sought after, and *inki* a condition of weakness to be overcome. See the discussion in Stoesz, ed., *Kurozumi Shinto,* 126f.
[89] One must remember that in Japanese context the dead are still affected by the living. But, an attached kind of "contact" does them no good.
[90] The concept of *dō, tao,* or "way" pervades Japanese culture. Examples familiar in the West are the art of flower arranging *(hana-dō)* or of tea ceremony *(cha-dō).* The German concept of *kunst,* "art" or "skill," is similar, but in Japanese understanding a "way" of doing something correctly may both connect the follower of that way with the order of things set in the cosmic scheme of things, and provide the inner integration needed for harmonious and happy life. When that happens, success in a utilitarian sense will inevitably follow.
[91] *"Kyōdan"* implies a religious society or "church" living by its own inner governance on a religious basis. Its religious basis does not necessarily have legal status. For further information see Hardacre, *Kurozumikyō and the New Religions of Japan,* 69.
[92] Author's note: Literally, rules *(sadame)* for the "Home of the Heavenly Heart" *(Tenshinsha),* as the lecture hall was called.
[93] Author's note: It had a broad spirit like that of Mahayana Buddhism, in contrast to other more narrowly conceived ideas of religious order and life.
[94] *Omoto-ke Hosokku; Kurozumikyō Kyōki.* That is, after the traditional Japanese manner, the rules for a whole social grouping would be set by the rules of its "head house" *(hon-ke);* in this case, that of the Kurozumi house *(ie).* On traditional Japanese social thought, see, for instance, Befu Harumi, *Japan: an Anthropological Introduction* (Tokyo: Charles E. Tuttle Company, 1981), 38ff.
[95] An intimate and empowering knowledge *(shiru)* of the heavenly presence is implied. According to Alan Grapard, the Yoshida Shinto tradition saw a connection between poetry and magical power, so that *waka* composed by one who was in a ritual state of purity could command the forces of nature. See *Encyclopedia of Japan,* 7: 131b. However, as Alan Miller has indicated, in Stoesz, ed., *Kurozumi Shinto,* 256, the deep kind of purity attained by the Founder was rather different in quality from that attained in ordinary Shinto purification. This version of this *waka* is by the editor, based on comments by Kurozumi Tadaaki and Kamiya Sumio.
[96] Ito Sadasaburō, *Memorandum of What I Have Seen and Heard (Kenbun Kikigaki).* See *Gonenpu,* 469; *Tales of the Founder,* 198. Ito's village was known as Matsuzaki at the time.
[97] The year, month, and day of the rat are the beginnings of these cycles of twelve respectively in the traditional calendar.
[98] They are usually given the respectful title of *sensei,* "teacher." In this translation, however, the term *Sensei* is reserved only for the Founder *(Kyōso),* to

emphasize his distinctive role. With the high disciples Ishio and Kawakami from the earlier period, Tokio and Akagi make up the Four High Disciples *(Kotei)*. As indicated below, the most trusted of all were given a name derived from the Teacher's name.

[99] At this time Christianity was still a forbidden faith in Japan. Popular belief in its negative character was often in accord with official government policy.

[100] The fourth line is a polite reference to the high-born members of the Imperial Court in Kyoto. The poem expresses Tokio's confidence that all may equally be knowers of the Sun Kami up to the Emperor himself, and his determination to act on that faith (English version by the editor.)

[101] Translation by Kamiya Sumio and Willis Stoesz.

[102] *"Daimyōjin"* is a rank and type of kami. The Yoshida family in Kyōto had been given the responsibility and right to regulate aspects of the religious life of the country, including the formal recognition of candidates for several kinds of kami. This rank carried with it permission to build a shrine and carry out enshrinement ceremonies. See Hepner, *The Kurozumi Sect*, 186ff. for details.

[103] Emended by the editor.

[104] *"Ikasu"* refers to a way of dealing with general situations so as to capitalize on favorable aspects and minimize unfavorable ones. A general policy of interaction is implied, based in confidence in Amaterasu both as the Kami of Heaven and Earth *(honshin)*, and as present within each human being *(bunshin)*. *"Ikasu"* is thus a specialized term in Kurozumi usage, expressing confidence in Amaterasu's enlivening effect in a process of human action open to her presence, and showing how individuals should interact with the particulars of their immediate contexts of action.

[105] *Kyōso Munetadashin Goshoden, Makoto no Kokorotsude, Michi no Shiori Sanjukajo, Hyakunijugen.*

[106] See Chapter 4.

[107] The title *Kyōshu* (Patriarch) was adopted in 1950 after State Shinto regulations of the early Meiji period had been abolished. When the Kurozumi *Kyōdan* was first given government recognition under those regulations, Muneatsu was accorded the title *Kanchō* or "supervisor." *Kyōshu* is a more congenial term, deriving from internal understanding of religious authority over the teachings, rather than from an externally imposed source. As the third in line from the Founder as head of the Kurozumi family, he was after 1950 reckoned the third *Kyōshu*. *Kanchō* is no longer used. See also Hepner, *The Kurozumi Sect*, 216f. There is only one *Kyōso*, or Founder. The present Chief Patriarch, Kurozumi Muneharu, is the sixth in succession from the Founder.

[108] English version by the editor.

[109] In Shinto belief, the "High Plains of Heaven" *(Takamagahara)*, a term already used in ancient mythology, is where purified kami rest after death. See Kurozumi Muneharu, "Following the Way," in Stoesz, ed., *Kurozumi Shinto*, 82-88, for Kurozumi teaching about the afterlife.

[110] Kurozumi followers understand that the unity of Munetada and Kami is made present to them in the daily movement of the sun, from morning *nippai* through all the simple or great events of each day. English version by the editor.

[111] These stories are taken from *Kyōso-sama no Itsuwa* (Okayama, 1974),

except as indicated. They have been selected by Kurozumi Tadaaki to give a better understanding of the character of the Founder. The translation is by Kamiya Sumio.

This edition number	Number in the original
1.	11.
2.	29.
3.	
4.	
5.	43.
6.	17. (Supplement)
7.	59.
8.	14.(Supplement)
9.	10. (Supplement)
10.	2.
11.	23.
12.	40.
13.	24.
14.	45.

[112] *I.e.*, Founder. The term will be left untranslated here in order to express in these stories the intimacy Kurozumikyō members feel toward him.

[113] The "eight million kami" *(yao yorozu no kami;* i.e., an uncountable number of kami) are the sum of those who have been created as "divided small souls *(bunshin)"* by Amaterasu. All are (equally, in Kurozumi thinking) the "divine child of Kami," all are one in Kami.

[114] Taken from *Kurozumikyō Kyōso Itsuwa-shu.* The same story occurs in Chapter Four, but here the text is more complete.

[115] This story, whose original text has been lost, is often retold in Kurozumi tradition. This is the author's telling of it.

[116] The dolls' festival is held each year on the third day of the third month, a very popular and happy time of the year. The platform has a series of shelves resembling a stairway, perhaps three or four feet high, with dolls representing a prince (always seated on their right) and princess, the attending samurai below them, then court ladies and musicians in descending order according to their rank in traditional society. A full set of such dolls is displayed in homes and in schools on the festival day.

[117] I.e., the *temizuya,* a covered place with running water where worshipers stop to rinse their hands and mouths before entering a shrine. It is a place of purification preparatory to worship.

[118] In earlier days when traditions were stronger than now, members of families in which a death had occurred were regarded as impure. Until a period of mourning was over — up to a year when it was a parent who had died — they were not allowed to visit public places that could be defiled by their presence. It is part of the Confucian heritage of Japanese culture.

Bibliography

I. Kurozumi Literature

A. *Kurozumikyō kyōsho,* ed. Kurozumi Muneyasu (Okayama: Kurozumikyō Nisshinsha, 1974). The *Kyōsho,* the official compilation of the teachings of Kurozumikyō, consists of the following:

1. *O-uta: Waka.* Poems composed by the Founder to convey his teachings;
2. *Gobun:* letters he sent to his followers; *Den Gobun:* those that survive only as copies;
3. *Zasshu: (Miscellany);* Munetada's diaries and accounts of his pilgrimages to Ise; memoranda, notes and comments on various things he experienced or heard; and other writings and documents of Munetada written from time to time;
4. *Michizure Toshi Oboedome: The Register of Followers,* including the traditional calendar year in which they were born, and, in the case of samurai, their rank as measured by their yearly stipends (in *koku* of rice);
5. *Monjin Nadokoroki: The Register of Disciples;* names and addresses of those who had given their vows *(shinmon):* the "Vowed Society" *(Shinmon Shū).*
6. *Gonenpu:* the *Chronology of The Founder's Life,* from birth to his ascension to the Heavens.

B. Other Kurozumi literature

"Akagi's Evening Talks." Copy of manuscript in Kurozumikyō Headquarters.
Biography. Kawakami Chūsho, *Biography of the Great Deity. (Munetada Daimyōjin Godenki).* Okayama: Kurozumikyō Nisshinsha, 1965.
Chronology of Kurozumi Documents. Kysho, pp. 413-482.
Denshu Kikigaki; Goshden Denshu Kikigaki. Notes by Miyake Juzo on lectures by Hoshijima Ryōhei on his book, the *Goshōden.*

Gokōden; Munetada Shin Gokōden (Memorandum of the Founder's Sermons and Letters). Jikihara Ihachiro. Okayama: moto Gakuen, 1965 (mimeographed).

Gokōshakuden. A compilation of notes made by various people on the Founder's lectures and sermons.

Kurozumi Church Regulations (Kurozumikyō Kyōki). Current name of a document frequently revised; originally prepared as "Kurozumikyō Kōsha Kisoku" ("Regulations for the Kurozumi Association"). All revisions on file at Kurozumikyō Headquarters.

"Memorandum of What I have Seen and Heard" *(Kenbundan Kikigaki).* Ito Sadasaburō (original preserved by the Ito family of Tottori Prefecture).

Nisshin. Okayama 1- (1914-). The journal was originally named *Kuni-no-Oshie (Teachings of the Nation),* renamed *Keisei Zasshi (Leading Your Life Magazine)* in 1909, and again renamed *Nisshin (The New Sun)* in 1914. It continues under that name.

"Omoto House Regulations" *(Omoto-ke Hosoku).* Preserved at Kurozumikyō Headquarters.

"Record of Gifts Received." *Kysho,* pp. 464-467.

"Rules for the Group Studying the Divine Teachings." Original rules for the *Tenshinsha* (Heaven-Heart Society) preserved at the Nagasaki Kurozumikyō Church.

Short Biography. Hoshijima Ryōhei, *Short Biography of our Founder (Kyōso Munetadashin Goshōden).* Okayama: Kurozumikyō Headquarters, 1877, and successive recent printings by Kurozumikyō Nisshinsha.

Tales of the Founder; *Kysōsama no oitsuwa,* ed. Komoto Isshi (Okayama: Kurozumikyō Nisshinsha, 1960. rev. ed, 1974). *Itsuwa* were first published in *Kuni-no-Oshie,* official journal of Kurozumikyō, in 1895. Other such stories were published subsequently from time to time. A total of 111 stories had accumulated by 1949, and were edited and published under the title *Kurozumikyō-no-Go Itsuwashu.* The 1974 edition is a shortened and edited version of the first edition, but in a supplement includes 25 stories not previously published.

"A Written Memorandum Concerning Missionary Work." *Kyōsho,* p. 427.

II. For further reading

Beardsley, Richard, *et al. Village Japan.* Chicago: University of Chicago Press, 1959.

Befu, Harumi. *Japan: An Anthropological Introduction.* Rutland, Vt. and Tokyo: Charles E. Tuttle Co., 1981.

Bellah, Robert. *Tokugawa Religion.* New York: The Free Press, 1985.
Davis, Winston. *Japanese Religion and Society; Paradigms of Structure and Change.* Albany: State University of New York Press, 1992.
Hall, John W. *Government and Local Power in Japan.* Princeton: Princeton University Press, 1966.
Hardacre, Helen. *Kurozumikyō and the New Religions of Japan.* Princeton: Princeton University Press, 1986.
— — — — — —. *Shinto and the State.* Princeton: Princeton University Press, 1989.
Hepner, Charles W. *The Kurozumi Sect of Shinto.* Tokyo: Meiji Japan Society, 1935.
Holtom, D.C. *The National Faith of Japan.* New York: Paragon, 1965.
Keene, Donald. *World Within Walls; Japanese Literature of the Pre-Modern Era, 1600-1867.* New York: Holt, Rinehart and Winston, 1976.
Kitagawa, Joseph. *On Understanding Japanese Religion.* Princeton: Princeton University Press, 1987.
— — — — — — —. *Religion in Japanese History.* New York: Columbia University Press, 1966.
Kodansha Encyclopedia of Japan, ed. Itasaka Gen et al. Tokyo: Kodansha International Ltd., 1983.
Murakami, Shigeyoshi. *Japanese Religion in the Modern Period,* trans. H. Byron Earhart. Tokyo: Tokyo University Press, 1980.
Nobuhara, Taisen. *The Brilliant Life of Munetada Kurozumi; A Philosopher and Worshipper of the Sun,* 2nd ed. Tokyo: PC Publications, Inc. 1982.
Nosco, Peter, ed. *Confucianism and Tokugawa Culture.* Princeton: Princeton University Press, 1984.
Ono, Sokyo. *Shinto: The Kami Way.* In collaboration with William P. Woodard. Rutland, Vt. and Tokyo: Charles E. Tuttle Co., 1962.
Sansom, George. *Japan: A Short Cultural History,* 2nd rev. ed. Stanford: Stanford University Press, 1978.
Stoesz, Willis, ed. *Kurozumi Shinto; An American Dialogue.* Chambersburg, Pa.: Anima Books, 1989.
Varley, H. Paul. *Japanese Culture,* 3rd ed. Honolulu: University of Hawaii Press, 1984.
Walthall, Anne. *Social Protest and Popular Culture in Eighteenth-Century Japan.* Tucson: University of Arizona Press, 1986.

Indices

(Bold face shows where to find definitions.)

I. Subjects

anger 58

Amaterasu

audience with 51, 81; children of 17, 31, 55; Creator xxiv, 21, 69; faith in xxii, 48, 54, 58, 65, 68, 74, 81; governs all xxii, 98; Great Kami (Ōmikami) xvii, xxii, 21, *passim;* greatest deity 21; heart of xxii, 22, **n.39**, 23, 25, 33, 48, 58, 65, 79, 98, 113, 116, 117; Heaven (and Earth) xxiv, **n.29**, 16, 19, 20f., 27, 35f., 44f., 46, 55, 63, 67, 79, 84, 93, 96f., 116; *honshin* (Cosmic Spirit) x, **n.29**, 43, n.104; intention *(Goshinryo)* xxiv, 22, **n.39**, 23; Kami of the Sun ixf, xi, xii, 2, 26, **19f.**, 98; Mother (Parent) xxiv, 20, 21, 48, 57; Round Spirit 20, 22, 65; unity with xii, 19ff, 21, 27, 59, 67, 70, 84; will of xxiv, 21, 55, 60; *yōki* of 21, 24, 66

ascetic practices *(see shugyō)*

asceticism **46f.**, 59

Buddhism viii, n.7, 4, 31, 33, 39, 46, 55, 69f., 78, 108

bunshin ("microcosm") ix, x, xviif, 10, **n.29.**, 26, 34, 43, 60, 66, 99, 103

calendar 1, **n.17**, 3, 40

Chinese classics 8f., 39, 81, 87, 88

Christianity vi, xviii, 82

classes of society xi, 2, 30, 31, 74, 86, 89, 102

"clouds" (faults) 20, **21f.**, 95

conceit *(manshin)* 10, 46, **58**, 82

Confucian scholars 39, 40, 41, 74, 87

Confucianism viii, x, xi, xii, xxiii, 4f., n.83, 69, 78f., 88

conscience 10

constancy of inner spirit 63f., 99

nen o tsugu 58

daiyōki ("spiritual power") 25, 38, 66

(see also yōki)

death ix, 20, 47, 92-94, 95, n.109, 115

Direct Bestowal of Divine Mission xxii, 11, 17, **19ff.**, 22, 23, 38, 47, 49, 52, 56, 60, 68

ecstatic utterance 26, 62, **n.82**, 60f.

emblem 51f.

equalitarianism 31, 100, 103

evil 68

(see also "clouds," hardship)

favor *(on)* 40, 87

filial piety xvii, xxiiif., 5, 7, 9, 12, 15, 16, 19, 23, 40f.

Five Articles 10f., 56

Followers

direct disciples 29, **35**, 75, 79; general members *(michizure)* xxi, 58, 73, **n.54**; inner group *(Tenshin shu)* 54; Grand Missionary Campaign 82, 85, 97; High Disciples: Two pillars *(kokumon)* 84; Four... 79, 87; Six... 79, 85, 87; meeting days *(kaijitsu)* **25f.**, 29, 34, 40; meetings 31; *Banchō* group 31, 89; vow, pledge *(shinmon)* 26, 34, **35**, 36-38, 58, 73, 75, 87, 89; Vowed Society 54

gratitude ix, 17, 19, 24, 27, 30, 36, 40, 44, 54, 56, **58**, 59, 65f., 67, 81, 84, 93, 95, 100, 101, 115

II. Persons and Places

About the Author

Kurozumi Tadaaki was born in Okayama, Japan in 1919. He graduated from Tokyo University in 1943 with a major in Occidental Philosophy, and then served as a teacher of English in the Japanese Navy. In 1945 he joined the Kurozumikyō headquarters staff in Okayama. In 1953 he became the Rector of the Kurozumikyō Institute, and also served as Head of several other Departments of the headquarters office. He was Director of the Educational Bureau and Chief Priest of the Munetada Shrine from 1981-1989. Since 1989 he has served as Vice Patriarch of Kurozumikyō.